THE STORY OF BREWING IN

BURTON
ON
TRENT

THE STORY OF BREWING IN

BURTON
ON
TRENT

ROGER PROTZ

The
History
Press

First published 2011

The History Press
The Mill, Brimscombe Port
Stroud, Gloucestershire, GL5 2QG
www.thehistorypress.co.uk

© Roger Protz, 2011

The right of Roger Protz to be identified as the Author
of this work has been asserted in accordance with the
Copyrights, Designs and Patents Act 1988.

British Library Cataloguing in Publication Data.
A catalogue record for this book is available from the British Library.

ISBN 978 0 7524 6063 5

Typesetting and origination by The History Press
Printed in Great Britain

CONTENTS

INTRODUCTION

It's known as Burton upon Trent, Burton-on-Trent or just plain Burton – but whichever title you choose, it's a remarkable place. At the height of its brewing powers, in the nineteenth century, the population was no more than 40,000 – and half of those Burtonians malted barley, manned mash tuns, coppers and fermenting vessels, built wooden casks, and transported beer by truck and train. For a time, Burton meant only one thing: brewing. It was Beer Town or, if you prefer Victorian hyperbole, Beeropolis. Enormous quantities of beer were made. Towards the end of the nineteenth century, Bass, the biggest brewer in the town, was producing more than 1 million barrels a year. It was, for a time, the biggest brewer in the world and Bass Ale was available not only throughout the British Isles but also in the farthest-flung corners of the empire, Europe and North America. Other famous names in Burton brewing – Allsopp, Salt and Worthington, to name just three – followed Bass into the export trade. Long before golden lager appeared from central Europe, the Burton brewers had harnessed the new technologies of the Industrial Revolution to make the pale ale that revolutionised brewing on a world scale.

But Burton is about more than pale ale and India Pale Ale. A different style of beer existed before them and it's been one of the many pleasures of writing this book to tease out the history of a stronger and sweeter beer known as Burton Ale that was also exported in large quantities and found favour at the court of the Russian Tsars. The town is steeped in brewing history, from the time of Burton Abbey, where the monks fashioned ale for domestic use, through the rise of small 'common' or commercial brewers to the veritable cornucopia of brewing in the nineteenth century.

The history of brewing in Burton is intertwined with the magical waters of the Trent Valley. As a result of large deposits of sulphates in the valley, mainly gypsum and magnesium, the mineral-rich spring waters bring out the finest flavours of

Above and below: towering piles of casks at Bass, Burton.

malt and hops during the brewing process. From the founding of the settlement that became Burton by an Irish nun – who used the local waters to cure the sick – to the modern day, Burton water is world-famous and brewers of ale everywhere speak of 'Burtonising' their local supply to replicate the waters from the valley of the Trent. In the nineteenth century, before scientists could adjust water to reproduce Burton 'brewing liquor', brewers from London, Liverpool and Manchester built second plants in the town to join the rush to make pale ale.

One of those 'foreign brewers', Peter Walker, developed a system of fermentation known as the Burton Union method, which enhanced the flavour and appeal of pale ale as drinkers were switching from pewter tankards to glass containers and demanded crystal-clear beer, free of yeast and dregs. I have attempted, with the aid of expert brewers, to show how both Burton Ale and India Pale Ale were brewed and what they may have tasted like in the eighteenth and nineteenth centuries.

In short, this book has been a voyage of discovery. It's not a full-blown history of the town, though the social underpinning of Burton cannot be ignored, but an attempt to trace the history of beer-making there. Most of the great names of the nineteenth and twentieth century have now gone – the result, in the main, of short-sightedness, short-termism and a Gadarene rush to make types of beer alien to the history of Burton. But the book ends on an optimistic note, as one large group and smaller craft producers restore Burton's true brewing traditions.

During my many visits to Burton while I was researching this book, I was shown generous support not only from brewers but also from local people happy to give me directions or point me to the right bus stop. Few of them work in the brewing industry today but they are aware of the town's heritage: nobody on the streets or in the pubs of Burton talk about Coors or the National Brewery Centre: they are 'Bass' and the 'Bass Museum'. Whom Bacchus has joined together, let no man put asunder.

When I booked in to a B&B on one trip, the owner said: 'I recognise your name. You write about beer, don't you?' When I asked him how he knew, he replied, 'I worked for Bass for thirty years' and then regaled me with memories of his time with the company. In common with all Burtonians, he is rightly proud of the town's great brewing past. I hope this book will underscore their pride and help point to a new future for good ale in Beer City.

Roger Protz,
St Albans, 2011

Special thanks

From the list of people who helped with research for this book, two people merit special thanks.

Cordelia Mellor-Whiting is the curator at the National Brewery Centre. She not only oversees the collection of artefacts in the centre but is also in charge of the Bass Archive, a vast collection of books, images and memorabilia detailing the history of the brewery. Cordelia gave me a free run in the archive, patiently answered my questions then helped search for photographs to help illustrate the book. My debt to her is enormous.

Eric Fower would win any Mastermind competition on the subject of Marston's. He worked as an accountant at Marston's, finishing as head accountant, and he has devoted his retirement to the history of the company. I had three long meetings with Eric, who then patiently corrected my many mistakes. If any errors remain, I shall be found hanging, with a Staffordshire knot, from a union cask at Marston's brewery.

Thanks also to: Lesley Sweeney at Marston's Visitor Centre; Michael Hurdle, former chairman of Marston's; Arthur Roe, historian of Burton Abbey, for checking my chapter on the subject; May Arthur of the Burton branch of the Campaign for Real Ale; Chris Bowen in the United States for help with Arctic Ale; James McCrorie of the Craft Brewers' Association for recreating authentic Burton Ale and India Pale Ale; and Durden Park Beer Circle for allowing me to reproduce recipes from *Old British Beers and How to Make Them*. My son, Adam Protz, helped with research on Burton Abbey. Charlie, Matthew and Nick Otley at Otley Brewery in Pontypridd, South Wales, worked tirelessly and with great enthusiasm to brew a modern Burton Ale for me.

All the brewers in Burton gave generously of their time and beer. I single out Steve Wellington at William Worthington's Brewery, who has been a friend for many years and who will have retired by the time this book is published. He deserves his retirement, for he has been a great brewer of good beer.

Finally, as always, thanks to my wife Diana who, for once, was sanguine about my long absences from home as her father, Len Hoose, was born in Burton, giving us a family connection with what has almost become my second home.

ALLSOPP & SONS UNION & STORE ROOMS.

BASS & Cos OFFICES & "OLD" BREWERY.

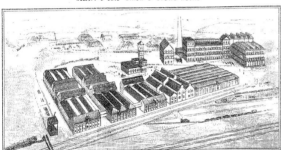

ALLSOPP & SONS "NEW" BREWERY AND MALTINGS.
(BIRDS EYE VIEW.)

BASS & COS. "NEW" BREWERY & MALTINGS.

ALLSOPP & SON'S OLD BREWERY.

BASS & CO.'S SHOBNALL MALTINGS.

Staffordshire Breweries (clockwise from top left): Allsopp & Son's Union Store Rooms; Bass and Co's offices and 'old' brewery; Allsopp & Son's 'new' brewery; Bass & Co.'s 'new' brewery; Allsopp and Son's 'old' brewery; Bass & Co.'s Shobnall maltings.

Chapter One

SAINTS AND SINNERS

The fame of Burton and its beers is an ancient one. In *Ivanhoe*, set in the twelfth century, Sir Walter Scott speaks lyrically of the fame of Burton ale, which, he says, predates the reign of Richard I (1157-1199). The ale at that time would have been brewed by the monks of Burton Abbey, though Scott in the novel calls it 'the convent of St Withold'. Beer and ale cannot be made without water, and Burton and the Trent Valley have long been renowned for the quality of what brewers call 'liquor'. Shakespeare's roots were in the Midlands and in *Henry IV Part One* he records Harry Hotspur, the Earl of Northumberland, bemoaning the scarcity of the land he owns in the area compared to that of the Welsh prince, Owen Glendower:

> Methinks, my moiety [share], north of Burton here,
> In quantity equals not one of yours;
> See, how this river comes me cranking in,
> And cuts me, from the best of all my land,
> A huge half-moon, a monstrous cantle [slice] out.
> I'll have the current in this place damm'd up,
> And here the smug and silver Trent shall run,
> In a new channel, fair and evenly;
> It shall not wind with such a deep indent,
> To rob me of so rich a bottom here.

Hotspur was well aware of the quality of the arable land bordering the Trent, irrigated by the river's 'silver' water. With remarkable prescience, the earl's talk of changing the course of the river chimes with later bridges and canals that opened

Burton Abbey – rear of the infirmary, alongside tributary of the Trent.

Burton Abbey – front of the infirmary, the last remaining building.

Burton and its beers to a world far beyond Staffordshire and Derbyshire. It was the Trent and its tributaries that would start Burton ale on a journey to towns and cities throughout Britain and on to Europe, the Baltic and Russia, and eventually to India, other parts of the British Empire and even North America.

Water was responsible for the founding of Burton, first known as Byrtune and by the time of the Domesday Book as Bertone. Is it fanciful to think that from its earliest days the very word beer was interwoven with the name of the town?

While a type of rough ale would have been made in the homesteads of the people, the Benedictine abbey of Burton was the first major brewer in the town and dominated local production until the Dissolution of the monasteries. The abbey was founded in 1002 by Wulfric Spott, the powerful Earl of Mercia and a leading member of the court of the notoriously unready king, Ethelred. Wulfric was the son of Wulfruna, who founded Wolverhampton, and they were descended from Alfred the Great, the King of Wessex in the ninth century. Anglo-Saxon Byrtune was also called Muddwennstow, which means the 'holy place of St Modwen' and, if the legends of the area are true, Alfred and his descendants owe their existence to the saint and the magical waters of the Trent Valley.

Modwena was an Irish nun who came to England with two companions, Athea and Lazar, while on a pilgrimage to Rome. They paused en route and built a chapel on an island in the Trent; they called the island Andressey or St Andrew's Isle. Modwena eventually travelled on to Rome but returned to England several times and in total lived on Andressey for seven years. A second church was consecrated on the banks of the Trent and was dedicated to St Peter and St Paul. The island became a place of pilgrimage and also a sanctuary for the sick. Modwena discovered a spring on the island with mineral-rich water that cured people suffering from a variety of diseases. King Ethelwolfe sent his son Alfred to Andressey to be cured of scurvy, which was thought to be incurable: scurvy and similar ailments were widespread at the time as a result of poor diet. Alfred was cured by Modwena and the nun also gave the future king a sound education. It was the powers of the water that enabled Alfred to live and to beget descendants who played a fundamental role in the development of Burton.

As for Modwena, she travelled as far north as Scotland to convert people to Christianity. She died in Scotland at the age of 130 – or so the legend goes – around the year 900. Her remains were sent for burial on Andressey and they were later moved to Burton Abbey by Wulfric Spott. She was elevated to the sainthood by public acclamation (a Papal decree was not necessary at the time) but when the abbey was dissolved the Shrine of St Modwen was destroyed. She is remembered today by St Modwen's, the parish church on Market Place, on the site of the abbey, and the Roman Catholic church of St Mary and St Modwen in Guild Street, just a few yards from the former Bass breweries. Sceptics may feel that no such person

St Modwen's, on the site of main Burton Abbey.

as Modwen ever existed and it stretches credulity to believe she lived to such a great age. But Abbot Geoffrey of Burton in the twelfth century made an arduous pilgrimage to Ireland to search for her origins and her story is recorded by Holinshed in his *Chronicles of England*.

The Abbey of St Benedict and All Saints quickly became one of the most important monasteries in England. It stood alongside a tributary of the Trent known as the Oxhay and occupied 14 acres of land. The abbot was also lord of the manor, had a seat in parliament and sat on royal commissions. During its life, the abbey had thirty-five abbots and their roll-call gives a fascinating insight into the change from the Anglo-Saxon period, through the Norman invasion to more recognisably modern English names. The first three abbots were called Wulfgeat, Brihtric and Leofric in the eleventh century. In the twelfth and thirteenth centuries the Norman influence can be seen in such names as Roger Malebranche and Richard de Lisle. In the fifteenth and sixteenth centuries, the abbots had the more familiar English names of John Sudbury, William Mathew, Ralph Henley, William Boston and, finally, William Edys or Edie, who surrendered the abbey in 1538.

The abbey was powerful but it was by no means rich – in fact, the monks complained it was the poorest monastery in England. It was frequently plagued by financial crises in spite of owning vast tracts of land bequeathed them by Wulfric, who died in 1010 in a battle with the Danes at Ipswich. Following a bad harvest, Abbot Leofric had to strip gold and jewels from the sacred shrine of St Modwen to buy supplies and alleviate famine. As time passed, the monks began to deviate from the simple life of work and prayer recommended by St Benedict. The abbot and his prior, and other leading monks, became a ruling elite, with their own substantial apartments where they entertained guests. The guests were not always of a strictly religious persuasion. Abbot John Sudbury, in particular, led a dissolute life and on several occasions was charged with adultery, entertaining women, and specifically with ravishing Margaret Taverner in his chambers on Christmas Day. (The name Taverner suggests the woman in question was an innkeeper.) He faced other charges of cattle rustling, poaching and common assault. He was pardoned by both Henry IV and V, who were anxious to keep the support of key abbots at a time when the country was divided by rebellions and insurrections, including those led by Owen Glendower in Wales. In the fifteenth century, Abbot Ralph Henley was reprieved on a charge of being an accessory to murder, but was later forced to resign as a result of persistent drinking. No doubt he had sought solace in the ale brewed for him by his monks or by innkeepers in the town. An ironic local rhyme of the time said:

The Abbot of Burton brewed good ale,
On Fridays when they fasted.
But the Abbot of Burton never tasted his own
As long as his neighbour's lasted.

Under the feudal system, peasants had to work two days of each week for the abbot, and also had to supply the abbey with their own produce. This included part of the grain they grew, which was ground in the abbey's mill and used for making bread and beer. The abbey buildings, first made of wood but replaced by red sandstone, included a brew house where the cellarer was a key member of the fraternity, responsible for supplying food and drink. The brew house, along with the stables, granary and infirmary, were outside the central cloisters; the monks there were able to employ lay people. While the number of monks at Burton never exceeded thirty, stewards, bailiffs, gatekeepers, domestic servants and general labourers created a substantial community of some 350 people. From humble beginnings, the tiny hamlet of Byrtune started to develop into a sizeable settlement.

The church's attitude to brewing was a complex one. Ale was a vital part of people's diets. Made from barley and other grains and fermented with yeast, it was rich in vitamin B that helped keep scurvy and other diseases at bay. Ale was of particular importance to monks during the strict fasting period of Lent: the monks called ale 'liquid bread', a term still used by monastic breweries in Belgium and Bavaria. Ale was safe to drink. Water, even from Hotspur's 'silver Trent', was polluted, and the monks of Burton would have used water from the many springs in the area. Crucially, water was boiled during the brewing process, killing bacteria.

But as well as vitamins and pure water, ale also contained alcohol, and the church elders were anxious to avoid the wild excesses of the Anglo-Saxon period.

Abbeys and monasteries therefore excised a near-monopoly over the production and availability of ale. The abbot's guests and pilgrims were offered ale and food in an attempt to prevent them visiting common ale houses. Ecbright, the Archbishop of York, instructed his bishops and priests in the eighth century to provide their own hospices for travellers and to supply them with home-produced victuals. He forbade priests under his jurisdiction from visiting ale houses, but it seems this rule was honoured more in the breach than the observance. In Burton the first recorded inn in the town was the Swan on the Hoop, which appears in a property deed of 1425. As common ale houses and inns spread, the Bishop of Lichfield and Coventry found it necessary, in 1498, to place a formal ban on the monks of Burton frequenting such low places.

The hierarchy of the abbey was keen to monopolise the supply of ale for sound commercial reasons. Soon after the abbey was founded, the monks started work on a bridge over the Trent. As a result, pilgrims were able reach the abbey with comparative ease. As abbey life changed, with the abbot, the prior and other key monks forming a ruling group, rich guests were made especially welcome. Spacious rooms were built to provide better accommodation than that offered to impoverished pilgrims, and the guests were plied with fine food and the best ale in return for generous payments. The abbot was keen to maximise his income: a document dating from 1295 records that 'Matilda, daughter of Nicholas de Shobenhale, released to the Abbot and Convent of Burton-on-Trent certain tenements and interests within and without the town: for which release they granted her daily for life two white loaves from the monastery, two gallons of the convent beer, and one penny besides seven gallons of beer for the men and other considerations.'

Large amounts of ale were consumed by the monks and their guests. The usual ration of beer, approved by the local bishop, was a gallon a day (eight pints) of 'small beer' for each monk. Small beer (a term used by Shakespeare in *Henry VI, Part Two*: 'I will make it a felony to drink small beer'), referred to a weak drink, the final washings of the brew, which was suitable for nursing mothers and children. It was less than 3 per cent alcohol in modern measurement. The buildings set aside for monastery breweries were enormous. Little remains of Burton Abbey but at Fountains Abbey in Yorkshire, the ruins of which still stand, the malt store alone measured 60sqft and the brewery produced sixty barrels of strong ale every ten days. The Domesday Book recorded that the monks of St Paul's in London brewed 67,814 gallons of beer a year, equivalent to 1,884 barrels. Barley, wheat and oats were used in the brewing process, but barley would have been the preferred grain. Some 3,000 years BC, when beer was first made in the Old World of Babylonia, Egypt and Mesopotamia, the ancients discovered, by trial and error, that barley made indifferent bread but excellent ale. But before beer can be made, grain has to be turned into malt to turn starch into fermentable sugar.

Monastic brewing was not confined to England. In the early Middle Ages there were between 400 and 500 monasteries brewing in Germany alone. Brewing at that time was remarkably sophisticated. Plans of the Abbey of St Gaul in Switzerland in the ninth century show a malt house, kiln, mill room for grinding malt and three brew houses and storage cellars. The maltings were large enough to allow four separate 'couches' or floors of grain to be processed at a time. When the grain started to germinate it was transferred to a kiln, a square structure with a central chimney around which were fixed wickerwork platforms covered with rough material. The germinated grain was spread on the material while heat from the kiln turned grain into malt. The kiln was fired by wood.

A detailed study of medieval monastic brewing in France in 1969 recorded that while barley, oats, rye and wheat were used, the monks preferred barley as it was easier to malt and also had a husk that acted as a filter during the brewing process. Grain was laid out in a cool cellar and then moistened with water to start germination. As in Burton, French monastic brew houses were placed close to rivers. Records of Clairvaux Abbey say that river power ground the corn, worked the sieves that separated flour from bran and provided water for cloth-making and tannery, and finally carried away the monks' refuse. In some breweries, the grain was spread on the ground overnight in secluded areas away from the wind so that the morning dew would moisten it. Malt was turned by hand to aerate it and when it started to sprout it was moved to a stone-built kiln and laid out on a thin floor covered with hair-cloth above a hearth. The progress of the transformation of barley into malt was marked by chewing it until it was friable in the mouth.

The monks in Burton had the ingredients to hand to make ale: malted barley and other grains, pure water (possibly from St Modwen's spring) and yeast. They would have had no scientific understanding of yeast – it remained a mystery until it was analysed by Louis Pasteur in the nineteenth century. English brewers in medieval times called yeast 'Godisgood' and they clearly thought that the violence of fermentation and the creation of alcohol were the work of the Almighty. Yeast would have been saved and re-used from one brew to the next. The brewing vessels in Burton Abbey no longer exist (though they survived for a while following the Dissolution: *see* the next chapter). But vessels from that period endured until the Second World War in Queen's College, part of Oxford University, and date from the founding of the college in 1340. The mash tun, the vessel in which malted grain is mixed with water, was made of Memel oak. It had two outlet pipes covered with metal strainers to contain the grain. The sweet liquid created by mashing grain and water is called wort and this flowed to an underback (or receiving vessel) below the tun, and was then transferred by hand to an open copper heated by a furnace. Hops would not have been used during the first century or two of the brewery's existence but boiling the wort was essential to killing any bacteria present.

Following the boil, the wort was cooled in large open pans made from deal and then, at 66 degrees Fahrenheit (18 degrees Celsius), transferred to a wooden vessel called a round where it was mixed with yeast. As soon as a vigorous fermentation started, the liquid was taken in a 'tun dish', a sort of large ladle, to casks in a cellar. The casks were arranged above a trough; as fermentation continued, yeast would froth out of the casks and was collected in the trough for future use. Once fermentation was complete, the casks were sealed and the ale left to mature. The strength of the ale was 1,070 degrees gravity, approximately 7 per cent alcohol by volume in modern measurement, twice the strength of an average British beer today. A Chancellor's Ale, double the strength and equivalent to a rich red wine, was also brewed from time to time.

This method of brewing was so widespread in the medieval period that it's safe to assume that similar vessels were used by the monks of Burton. The major difference between ale of that time and today is the absence of hops. The hop plant was a late arrival in England, brought to Kent by Flemish weavers in the fifteenth century who preferred beer with hops to unhopped ale. Today, all beer, almost without exception, is made with hops, whether it's lager beer or British-style ale. But in fifteenth-century England the terms 'ale' and 'beer' not only marked a clear division between the styles, but also were the cause of considerable controversy. The Romans in Britain grew hops and ate them as a delicacy, rather like asparagus, but the plant was not used in brewing. Following the break-up of the Roman Empire and the migration of people to northern Europe, knowledge of the hop's role in brewing was taken into parts of Germany by the Slavs. Hop gardens were recorded in the Hallertau region of Bavaria in AD 736. In 1079 the Abbess Hildegarde of St Ruprechtsberg, near Bingen, referred to the use of hops in brewing. Hop cultivation was also reported at the time in Prague, already emerging as an important brewing centre.

Since the earliest days of beer making, brewers attempted to balance the biscuity sweetness of malt with plants, herbs and spices. Hops were grown in Babylon around AD 200 and were being used in brewing from the eighth century. Brewers discovered the almost magical qualities of the hop that set it apart from other plants. Hop resins include acids and tannins that give an enticing aroma to beer and a quenching bitterness, and also prevent bacterial infection. Boiling the sugary extract, wort, with hops, especially when water was insanitary, became an important stage of the brewing process. But in every European country, the hop had to fight a long war of attrition with the old methods of brewing. The church resisted the use of hops because it controlled what was called the 'gruit market'. Gruit, also known as grut or gruut in different parts of Europe, referred to herbs and spices used in brewing that could only be bought from the church. In Cologne, the archbishop cornered the gruit market through a decree called the Grutrecht and he attempted to outlaw the use of hops, while in Russia Archduke Vassili II

Hops give aroma, flavour and bitterness to beer.

forbade their use. But as feudalism came under attack during the Renaissance, commercial brewers in such major centres as Amsterdam, Bremen and Hamburg began to switch to hops. The church responded by attempting to impose punitive taxes on the plant. Peace was only achieved when the religious authorities agreed to accept rents in lieu of giving up their rights to supply gruit.

There was fierce resistance to hops when they finally made an appearance in England. The plant was banned in Norwich, even though many Flemish weavers settled there. In 1519, the use of the 'wicked and pernicious' weed was prohibited in Shrewsbury while Henry VIII instructed his court brewer not to use hops: curiously, given later events during Henry's reign, his opposition to the hop was based on the plant's unpopularity with many English drinkers, who considered hopped beer to be a 'Protestant drink'. But the old order and attitudes were fighting a losing battle. Hop gardens were laid out in Kent in 1520 and the use of the plant spread as commercial brewing challenged the hegemony of the church and the rigidity of the feudal system. But the use of plants and herbs did not immediately disappear. In 1588, Theodor von Bergzabern, describing contemporary brewing practice in Europe, noted that hops were used in the copper boil but added: 'The English sometimes add to the brewed beer, to make it more pleasant, sugar, cinnamon, cloves and other good spices in a small bag.'

The seventeenth-century naturalist Dr Robert Plot (1640-1696), a member of the Royal Society, Professor of Chemistry at Oxford University and first Keeper of the Ashmolean Museum, wrote several studies of English counties, including *A Natural History of Staffordshire* in 1686. As well as discussing the chemical or natural properties of Burton water (which suggests the special nature of water in the Trent Valley was becoming established), he went on to say about Burton ale, 'We must also remember they have an art in this county of making good ale, which being a liquid and nothing else but boyled water, impregnated with mault, must be referred thither. In the management of which they have a knack of fineing [clearing] it in three days to that degree that it shall not only be potable, but as clear and palatable as one would desire any drinke of this kind to be.' Plot adds that in the Burton area, brewers frequently used '*Erica vulgaris* (heath) or ling instead of Hopps to preserve their beer, which gave it no ill taste; and that they sometimes here make mault of oats, which, mixed with that of barley, is called dredge mault; of which they make an excellent fresh, quick sort of drink.'

King James I passed through Burton in 1619 on his way to Tutbury (where his mother, Mary Queen of Scots, had been held prisoner). According to Sir Oswald Mosley in his *History of Tutbury,* written in the nineteenth century, the churchwarden of Barton-on-Needwood recorded in his account of the visit: 'Paid for carriage of the butter to Burton, and money that they spent that did carry it, 1s 4d. Alsoe spent in goinge to Barton to pay for malt and hops, and hay and oats, and the rest of the things, 6d.' Some eighty years

Part of the remains of Tutbury Castle.

after the dissolution of Burton Abbey, it's clear that hops had been adopted by brewers in Staffordshire. According to *A Victorian History of the Counties of England*, the earliest evidence of hops being used in Burton was the mid-1550s. Even if, towards the end of the abbey's life, the brewers may have begun to use the hop, they would certainly have continued to incorporate herbs and spices as well, a habit that continued for several centuries. The modern Nethergate Brewery in Suffolk, when it was recreating a London Porter beer, discovered a recipe from a brewery in the eighteenth century that used coriander and bog myrtle as well as hops. Nethergate also brews an Augustinian Ale in co-operation with Clare Priory, the mother house of Augustinian friars in the English-speaking world.

It's possible to sample gruit beer by visiting the brewery and restaurant Gruut in the Belgian city of Ghent, which once had ten monastic brew houses. Anninck De Splenter, who would have been called a brewster in medieval times, uses no hops in any of her beers, which range from gold to black in colour. Instead she infuses her brews with the likes of aniseed, bog myrtle, caraway seeds, cinnamon, ginger, heather, juniper berries, mugwort, myrica, rosemary, sage and yarrow. (Gruut, 10 Grote Huidevettershoek, 9000 Ghent.) They are not only a fascinating interpretation of an ancient beer style but also fine-tasting, refreshing beers in their own right.

While no recipes remain from the time of Burton Abbey, it's safe to assume that the brewers there followed the style of other monastic brew houses. The strength of the brews was marked on casks with crosses: the stronger the ale, the greater the number of crosses. The crosses were also a blessing in the hope that each brew would be good to drink and had not turned sour. Documents from the ninth century show that monasteries and their breweries reflected the growing stratification of society. The monks brewed the strongest and finest ale, *prima melior*, for the abbot, his entourage and distinguished visitors, a second brew, *secunda*, for themselves and their lay workers, and a weak *tertia* for poor pilgrims who came in search of bed and sustenance. The method of producing ale, which survived for many centuries, was to use just one mash of grain: the first mash would produce a strong ale, the second a common ale and the final one a small or weak ale considered fit for women and children as well as impoverished pilgrims.

No doubt the quality of monastic ale varied from abbey to abbey. But English ale enjoyed a good reputation. In 1158, Thomas Becket took chariot loads of casks of ale with him on a diplomatic mission to France 'decocted from choice fat grain as a gift for the French who wondered at such an invention – a drink most wholesome, clear of all dregs, rivalling wine in colour and surpassing it in savour.'

Becket, who became Archbishop of Canterbury and was murdered in the cathedral, brewed ale for the abbot of St Albans Abbey in Hertfordshire as a young priest. He left a fine brewing legacy. During the Peasants' Revolt of 1381, the abbey was besieged by supporters of Wat Tyler and John Ball. They agreed to leave only when the abbot plied them with copious amounts of his ale.

Burton Abbey was fortunate to survive the Dissolution. Many religious institutions were not only closed down by Henry VIII and Thomas Cromwell but were also substantially wrecked. When Abbot William Edys surrendered the abbey in 1540, it was turned into a collegiate church, with Edys as dean, but after just five years the former abbey and its substantial land holdings were handed by Henry to his secretary Sir William Paget; his descendants continued to dominate life in Burton until the nineteenth century. While all signs of Popery were destroyed, including the shrine of St Modwen, the buildings were initially left intact. They included the brew house, which continued to play a critical role in a drama in and around Burton in the sixteenth century.

Chapter Two

Beer and the
Babington Plot

One of the great tragedies of English history unfolded close to Burton. It involved a brewer in the town who was part of a plot fashioned at the highest levels of the Elizabethan state to bring about the death of Mary Queen of Scots. In 1585, Mary was transferred to Tutbury Castle, near Burton, where she had previously been held prisoner in 1569. She detested Tutbury more than any of the places where she had been imprisoned. As a result of her long incarceration – it lasted in total for nineteen years – her health was poor and it deteriorated rapidly at Tutbury. The heavily fortified castle stands on a hill on the edge of Derbyshire and Staffordshire. Mary complained that the castle was damp and the wind whistled into her chamber through the thin walls made of plaster and wood. Outside, a large midden that stored the waste from the castle gave off a terrible stench.

To make matters worse, Mary's jailer, Sir Amyas Paulet, was a strict Puritan who detested everything the Catholic Mary stood for. He felt she deserved her poor health and he refused to allow her to leave the castle to take exercise and to breathe fresh air away from the noxious midden. Paulet had been appointed to his post by Sir Francis Walsingham, Elizabeth I's Secretary of State, who ran an elaborate spy ring dedicated to hunting down enemies of the queen. Walsingham had left England during the reign of Mary Tudor and lived in France. On his return and subsequent elevation to high office, he persecuted Catholics with a zeal that matched Mary Tudor's witch-hunt of Protestants.

Elizabeth, through the prism of history, is revered as a tough and fearless monarch. Tough, yes, but she was certainly not without fear – and with good reason. She ran, with Walsingham, an elaborate authoritarian state in which it was advisable to toe the Protestant line, even if you were a celebrated playwright such as William Shakespeare. He was baptised a Catholic but found it convenient to please Elizabeth and the Tudor ascendancy. In *Richard III,* Shakespeare gave – to say the least – an exaggerated account of Henry Tudor's claim to the throne. Elizabeth's claim was equally tenuous. She was the daughter of Anne Boleyn and, as a result, was considered by Catholics – who included some of the most powerful and influential aristocratic families in England – to be illegitimate. They argued she should be replaced by the next in line, Mary Queen of Scots, her Catholic cousin. Elizabeth was excommunicated by the Pope and expected at any time an invasion from Europe led by the Spanish to topple her. It was therefore not surprising that the state machine was geared to defending her and to hunting down her opponents with the utmost severity.

Elizabeth's 'dear cousin' Mary was not a hapless bystander to these events. She was in constant touch with her supporters both in England and in Europe via the French Embassy in London. She eagerly sought news of the campaigns to free her and to place her on the throne. When letters and messages were denied her by Paulet, first at Tutbury and then at Chartley – a nearby manor house owned by the Earl of Essex, where she was moved in 1585 – she became the victim of an elaborate plot fashioned by Walsingham, one that involved an eager brewer in Burton. (A move to Burton rather than Chartley was vetoed by Walsingham on the grounds that Mary could make her escape down the Trent, while Chartley had a moat.) Walsingham had prepared the ground to ensnare Mary with the catch-all Bond of Association, passed by parliament in 1584. This chilling piece of legislation stipulated that a plot had only to be made in favour of Mary, rather than by her, for her to merit the death penalty.

Walsingham's determination to eliminate Mary can be seen in a letter he wrote to the Earl of Leicester: 'As long as that devilish woman lives neither Her Majesty must take account to continue in quiet possession of her crown, nor her faithful servants assure themselves of safety of their lives.' The Secretary of State planned to bring Mary down with two inter-related conspiracies that made up the Babington Plot. One was the assassination of Elizabeth; the second was a ploy to rescue Mary from captivity. Both conspiracies needed the support of a foreign invasion from Spain and other Catholic countries. Mary's complicity in these plots required written evidence, and so it was necessary to allow letters to be smuggled in to her at Chartley and for her replies to be taken out. The conduit for this correspondence was a brewer who supplied both Tutbury Castle and Chartley with beer. There is some confusion concerning his name. In 1584, Sir Ralph Sadler, the governor of

Tutbury Castle, wrote to Walsingham and asked: 'What place neere Tutbury beere may be provided for Her Majesties' use?' Walsingham replied that 'beere may be had at Burton three myles off; and if Mr Henry Cavendish's brewhouse in Tutbury may be borrowed, sufficient quantity of beere may be brewed there, and so the country much eased in caryage.' While it seems odd that Sadler was unaware of the presence of Cavendish in Tutbury, Walsingham's reply suggests that the Tutbury brewer could be used to supplement beer produced in Burton by a brewer named William Nicholson, who used the equipment in the outbuildings of the former abbey. Tutbury Castle would have needed considerable quantities of beer, for while Mary was a prisoner she was permitted a retinue of ladies-in-waiting, secretaries and servants. In Burton, the abbey had become a manor house owned by Sir Thomas Paget. Paget was a devout Catholic and he also knew Anthony Babington, the man at the centre of the plot to release Mary and place her on the throne.

Paget's father, Sir William, had been granted the abbey's lands by Henry VIII and Thomas Cromwell; he had held high office under Henry. During the regency council of Edward VI, led by Edward Seymour, the Duke of Somerset, Paget was made a Knight of the Garter and created Baron Paget of Beaudesert. When Somerset was toppled, Paget was briefly held in the Tower of London but was released the following year and appointed Lord Privy Seal by Mary Tudor. He discretely retired from public life when Elizabeth came to the throne. Thomas Paget's outspoken opposition to Elizabeth led to him being attainted in 1589 and his title was forfeited. The knighthood was restored in 1604 to his son, who had wisely converted to the Protestant cause.

Walsingham's plot was now ready to be enacted. He employed a double agent, Gilbert Gifford, to ensnare Mary. Gifford was a Catholic from Chillington in Staffordshire who, under interrogation by Walsingham – which would not have been pleasant, with threats of the rack and the thumbscrew – was 'encouraged' to act for the state. He presented himself to the French embassy in London where he was told there was considerable correspondence waiting for Mary. Before she came under the stern control of Paulet, Mary had received letters and notes that were smuggled in to Tutbury by laundresses employed in the castle. Paulet swiftly put an end to this lax behaviour. From then on, the only correspondence that reached the queen was sanctioned by Walsingham and his agents.

In London, diplomats at the French embassy, who lacked the conspiratorial skills of the English secret service, had some doubts about Gifford, who lodged with Thomas Phelippes, one of Walsingham's main agents and an expert decipherer of codes. In spite of these misgivings, the French entrusted Gifford with Mary's correspondence, and the die was cast. Gifford took the letters to Burton, where he stayed in an inn and passed the correspondence to the brewer, Nicholson. Walsingham, the perfect spy master, never named either Cavendish or Nicholson again and carefully referred to 'our honest brewer' in Burton. To her joy, Mary learned at Chartley that the brewer who supplied ale to the manor house and carried away the empty casks would bring letters to her and take away her replies for dissemination to her supporters.

Mary's secretary, Claude Nau, took down her letters from dictation and turned them into code. He wrapped the letters in a leather packet and handed it to Nicholson, who rolled the packet and slipped it through a cork tube in to the bung hole of the cask. The brewer returned to Burton, where he passed the packet to Gifford who took it to London and gave it to Phelippes. He deciphered the letters and sent them by express riders to Walsingham. When the Secretary of State had read them and had them copied, he returned them to Gifford, who, in his guise as an honest agent of Mary's, delivered them to the French embassy for onward transmission to France.

The plot was in place: now all Walsingham needed was, in modern terms, a 'fall guy'. He was Sir Anthony Babington, twenty-five years old, a devout Catholic squire from Dethick in Derbyshire. He was rich, with an annual income of £1,000, and he gathered round him a group of fellow young Catholics who were devoted to Mary, and who were fired by an increasing antagonism to Elizabeth. This antagonism was fuelled by their contacts in Europe, where Mary was considered a martyr to her faith. Babington in particular was promised lavish aid by Bernadino de Mendoza, a former Spanish ambassador to England. With astonishing indiscretion, Babington and his group spread wild rumours that a large European army was being assembled to invade England, topple Elizabeth and put Mary on the throne. Mary heard – or was allowed to hear – that Babington was championing her cause and sent him a note in one of Nicholson's empty ale casks. The note was duly read by Walsingham and then passed to Babington. He sent Mary, via Gifford and Nicholson, a long letter in which he outlined plans for an invasion from Europe to be joined by 'a strong party at every place' of English Catholics. The invasion would lead to the deliverance of Mary and the 'dispatch of the usurping Competitor'. Babington gave full details of all the stages of the campaign, including the highly incriminating information that the 'usurping Competitor' would be killed by six noble gentlemen drawn from Babington's close associates.

Mary replied to Babington, with the aid of one of the honest brewer's empty casks, approving his plans. Her letter included the sentence, 'Orders must be given that when their design has been carried out I can be *quant et quant* got out of here' – 'design' meaning the assassination of Elizabeth. In separate letters to supporters, Mary made it clear that action by the Spanish king was vital to the success of the enterprise. When Phelippes decoded Mary's letter to Babington, he sent it on to Walsingham with a macabre drawing of a gallows. The noose was tightening but, in order to put Mary's downfall beyond doubt, Walsingham added a forged postscript to the letter that had Mary asking Babington for the names of the 'six gentlemen' who would kill Elizabeth.

The plot quickly unravelled. When Babington heard that one of Mary's staunchest supporters, August Ballard, had been arrested, Babington hid in St John's Wood, north of London, until he was seized and taken to the Tower of London, where he confessed to Walsingham. Mary was unaware of Babington's arrest and thought the plan to free her had succeeded when, in August 1587, Paulet at Chartley, with unprecedented kindness, suggested she might care to ride out from the manor house and enjoy a hunt. When she saw a group of horseman approaching she thought her liberation was at hand – but her joy was short-lived. The horsemen were led by an emissary of Elizabeth, Sir Thomas Gorges, who told Mary she had conspired against the queen. Mary was sent to Fotheringay Castle in Northamptonshire, staying the night en route in Burton, where the brewer had helped in her downfall. At Fotheringay, Mary was tried and executed, while in London Babington's group were killed in two batches. The first batch, which included Babington, were hanged, cut down while still alive, disembowelled and then quartered. The savagery of their executions caused such an outcry that Elizabeth intervened and ordered that the second group should be allowed to die on the scaffold before they were cut down.

Nicholson prospered as the brewer and carrier of messages. He was paid twice for his work, by Paulet and Walsingham, plus the cost of his beer. He understood the value of his work and at one stage demanded an increase in pay from Paulet; the 'honest brewer' was clearly an early harbinger of the new market economy destined to replace feudalism.

The beer Nicholson made in Burton for Tutbury and Chartley marked the last known use of the vessels installed by the monks of Burton Abbey. The Paget family had made Beaudesert House in Cannock Chase their main home. The former abbey became a ruin, with stone and timber taken for building work elsewhere. Between 1719 and 1726, a new church was built on the site. Two old buildings remained for a while, known as the Manor House and Infirmary, but they were eventually turned into a pub called, with due respect to the history of the place, the Abbey Inn. But, with astonishing insensitivity, it has recently been refashioned as a restaurant and bar called The Winery. Nevertheless, the ancient buildings should be visited. The view from the rear, alongside a tributary of the Trent called the Oxhay, is breathtaking and a vivid reminder of the roots of brewing in Burton.

TRUMAN. HANBURY. BUXTON & CO! BREWERY.

THOMPSON & SONS BREWERY.

PETER WALKER'S (TRUSTEES) BREWERY.

WORTHINGTON & CO! BREWERY.

HILL & SONS BREWERY.

BELL & CO! BREWERY.

MARSTON & SON'S BREWERY.

Staffordshire Breweries (from top): Truman, Hanbury, Buxton and Co.'s Brewery; Thompson & Son's Brewery; Peter Walker's (Trustees) Brewery; Worthington & Co.'s Brewery; Hill & Son's Brewery; Bell & Co. Brewery; Marston & Son's Brewery.

Chapter Three

THE BALTIC BECKONS

Burton-on-Trent in the seventeenth century was a poor place. It was savagely and repeatedly fought over during the English Civil War. Based in the centre of the country, it was considered a place of strategic importance by both Parliamentarians and Royalists, with easy access across the bridge over the Trent. The town changed hands eight times before the war ended and Oliver Cromwell took control of the country. Such was the parlous state of Burton that fairs and markets were abandoned and the first flowering of commerce in the town came to an abrupt end. In the 1650s, the High Sheriff of Derby, Sir Simon Degge, reported: 'It was before the last wars a town much given to clothing, their kersies [woollen coats] being in great esteem in this country, but since the war has declined in trade, having suffered much by the plunder, it being held out against the king.' Reports at the time commented on the poverty of the people. One report in 1694 described Burton as 'very much ruined and decayed, its buildings and the inhabitants in general much impoverished.'

Many citizens were said to be 'on the parish' – in receipt of poor relief – and, as a mark of their indebtedness to the town, had to wear a pauper's badge on their sleeve. They forfeited their relief if they failed to attend church while those employed in the workhouse – which included children as young as five years old – had to work from five in the morning until nine at night, spinning or knitting. As a sign of the changing economic imperatives, the workhouse was expected to make a profit. One leading citizen who served as overseer of the poor was a church warden and town master named Benjamin Printon. He was a brewer, the first commercial beer-maker in the town. (It could be argued that Nicholson, the brewer who supplied beer to Tutbury Castle, was a commercial brewer but it's likely he used the brewing equipment from the abbey to mainly supply his own ale house in Burton.)

Trade started to revive. Even though the monarchy was restored following Cromwell's Protectorate, manufacture everywhere was challenging and replacing a feudal system based on ownership of land. In Burton, wool and cloth again became important trades and they were joined by the smelting of iron, nail making and the production of sacks and ropes made from hemp yarn. And, slowly at first, a small brewing industry started to develop, enabling Burton ale to gain a fine reputation beyond the confines of the town. Before Benjamin Printon arrived, publican brewers were expanding the scope of their trade. By 1600 there were forty-six licensed victuallers – publicans who brewed on the premises. Some of them started to export casks and bottled beer to London. The beer went to Hull via Derby and then on to the capital by boat. By the middle of the seventeenth century, a rudimentary road transport system took beer to London. Transport costs were high and made Burton beer expensive but it acquired a cult status among the wealthy in London.

The roads around Burton were in such a bad state of repair that it took three or four times as many animals to haul wagons than in better areas. The quality of the roads was improved by an Act of Parliament in 1663, which created turnpikes paid for by tolls, but transport in winter remained difficult when roads were often reduced to mud. The state of the roads created a particular problem for Burton's brewers as they were unable to produce beer in the summer as a result of high and uncontrollable temperatures. The cold season was of great importance to them. Salvation lay with the River Trent, as it allowed Printon – and the commercial brewers who followed him – to build their trade.

Printon came from Wapping in east London. He settled in Burton when he married a local woman, Maria Bannister. At first he struggled to be accepted in a rural backwater, where he was seen as a 'foreigner', but by dint of hard work in the community he became a respectable member of local society. The date is uncertain but it's thought he arrived in Burton in 1708 and opened a brew house in Bridge Street. Unlike the publican brewers in the town, he ran a brewery that was not connected to an inn, making him the town's first accredited commercial beer maker.

The Trent Navigation Act of 1699 aimed to make the river navigable from Burton to Shardlow. The 6th Baron Paget agreed, with other landowners, to allow work to take place on their properties, including part of the old abbey site. Paget paid half the costs, with the rest raised by the town authorities. Work was painfully slow until it was handed over to a Derbyshire businessman, George Hayne. In 1712, the Trent Navigation Co. started the work that eventually made the Trent navigable to Gainsborough and Hull. A port was built with a warehouse and wharf and, when the river had been dredged, shallow ketches were able to make the return trip to Gainsborough in twelve days. Seven thousand tons of goods, including ale, coal, metal goods, iron, timber, hemp and flax, were shipped annually by 1750. In 1777 the opening of the Grand Trunk Canal – better known as the Trent and Mersey Canal – through Burton completed a link between Liverpool and Hull, and gave added impetus to the Burton brewers, who were able to sell their beer throughout central and northern England and from Hull to London. The driving force behind the canal was Josiah Wedgwood, a potter from Burslem, Stoke-on-Trent, who was looking for fresh markets for his products. His initiative was further evidence of the way entrepreneurs were reshaping the commercial landscape. As a result of Wedgwood's efforts, the waterways offered Burton brewers their own route to bigger markets.

Burton ale was in demand in such leading London taverns as the Peacock in Gray's Inn Lane and the Dagger Inn in Holborn. By the early eighteenth century, there were references in London journals to 'Hull ale' and the diarist Samuel Pepys acquired a liking for what he also called Hull beer. But this was almost certainly beer from Burton that had reached the east coast port by way of the Trent and was then taken to London by boat. In 1712, 638 barrels of Burton beer passed through Hull en route for London and Joseph Addison noted in the *Spectator* that year, 'We concluded our walk with a glass of Burton ale'. The same journal reported that Burton beer was in great demand in Vauxhall Pleasure Gardens. An advertisement in the *Derby Mercury* in 1784 for the sale of a small brewery in Burton referred to the town's 'centrical situation' with 'communication with every capital Sea Port in the Kingdom'. To prove the point, the Trent and Mersey Canal was eventually linked to the Coventry and Oxford canals and from there to the Thames and London.

The roads were not ignored. Improvements to the turnpikes lead to a growth in the number of road carriers taking goods from Burton and Derby to London. Six wagons a week were leaving Burton for London by the 1760s. Among those plying for trade in the Burton area was a carrier called William Bass. Pubs acted as pick-up points for the wagons and the Crown, George and Three Tuns developed into sizeable coaching inns with stabling for horses. Lighter and faster coaches delivered mail and goods to London, while Burton was a stopping-off point for what was euphemistically called 'a special coach service' from London to Liverpool – it took prisoners who were being transported to Australia.

The town was no longer impoverished but was a thriving commercial centre. Businesses were looking beyond the shores of Britain for trade, and the river and canal links to Hull meant that Burton-made textiles, iron, rope and beer could be sent to the Baltic States, Scandinavia and Imperial Russia. Peter the Great and the Empress Catherine developed a liking for nut brown Burton ale, which was brewed strong – around 11 or 12 per cent alcohol – and well hopped to withstand the long sea journey. It remained in sound, drinkable condition for some seven months. Burton ale encouraged Czar Peter to help create a modern brewing industry in St Petersburg: before his time, brewing was a largely rural and domestic activity in Russia.

The Baltic trade brought new entrants to brewing in Burton. Although the water of the Trent Valley had yet to be scientifically analysed, brewers and potential brewers were aware that beer of a special quality could be made in the town. They were also keen to take part in the export and import of other goods with the Baltic, for brewing remained a seasonal activity between October and April. For example, Benjamin Wilson Junior not only brewed ale but dealt in timber, tallow, wheat, hemp, flax and iron. He sold on timber and imported wheat to other brewers in the Burton, Derby and Nottingham area. In some cases, no money changed hands – beer would be exchanged for timber and other imports. But that element of the trade never amounted to more than 25 per cent of the total and so much gold poured in to Burton that some of the new breed of brewers turned to banking. William Worthington became a banker in the town as well as running one of the leading beer-making businesses. John Walker Wilson, a brother of Benjamin Wilson Junior, left the family company to launch his own independent brewery: Walker Wilson was the leading timber merchant in the area, formed the Burton Bank in partnership with a local solicitor and became the richest of the three Wilson brothers.

All the new brewers became heavily involved in importing timber and staves from mainland Europe, the Baltic and Russia: so much English oak had been used to build ships, including men o' war, that there was a serious shortage of wood to make casks for beer. Oak from Poland in particular was in great demand in Burton and continues to be used by Marston's to build and repair the casks used in their union rooms to this day. But beer was the mainstay of the brewers' business and the trade was well organised. In the case of Wilson, his beer was transported by barge from Horninglow – the closest shipping point on the canal to Burton – to Gainsborough. There the beer was transferred to schooners owned by John Smith and taken to Hull, from where it left for the Baltic. Wilson had agents in Amsterdam, Danzig and Hamburg and in 1791 he sent a letter to his customers announcing he had taken on an assistant who was 'well acquainted with the German and Dutch languages to facilitate his correspondence in Consequence of the great increase of my foreign Friends for some years past.'

The rush to brew was on. Samuel Sketchley came from Newark in 1740: he opened a brewery in Horninglow Street and expanded in 1761 by buying part of the brewing business run by John Musgrave. Musgrave in turn had bought Printon's brew house in 1729 and enlarged the site. Joseph Clay from Derby bought the Lamb and Flag Inn in Horninglow Street; his interest was in the brewing side, not the inn.

Charles Leeson, a chandler, followed a similar course when he purchased the Three Queens in 1753. Henry Evans moved from Derby to set up a brewery in the High Street in 1754. William Worthington, a cooper from Orton-on-the-Hill in Leicestershire, worked at Joseph Smith's brewery in the High Street and bought Smith out in 1760. But far and away the most important brewer in the town in the eighteenth century was Benjamin Wilson, who established a dynasty that was to play a leading role in expanding sales of Burton ale and then, as Allsopps, developing trade with India.

Benjamin Wilson was a rope maker from Derby. He married Hannah Walker, owner of the Blue Stoops pub in Burton, and he took over the business in 1742, abandoning the pub in order to concentrate on brewing. His son, Benjamin Wilson Junior, developed the company into the biggest and most influential in the town. As well as exporting beer, Wilson had a growing local market to please. In the 1770s, a Lancashire cotton maker, Robert Peel – known as 'Parsley Peel' – opened mills in Burton and harnessed the water of the Trent for power.

It was employment in the mills that led to the town's population growing by a quarter between 1789 and 1801: the number stood at 4,667 in the latter year. Wilson, as the biggest brewer in Burton, was already chafing at the bit as the technologies of the late eighteenth century held the company back. In a letter dated 1791 to a customer in Elbing in Germany, Wilson said:

> From the unusual impatience of the Shipowners and Masters to depart so early in the Spring, I ought to begin to brew before the Winter sets in; but let me tell them and all whom it may concern that it would be very dangerous to the preservation of the ale, which is a material object both for me and my friends to consider. I commonly begin to brew in the beginning of November, and am not willing, notwithstanding the importunity of the shipowners, to open my winter business sooner.

Brewing in Burton, as the century drew to a close, was still a seasonal affair. Wilson complained that even a mild winter could force him to suspend brewing as he could not control mashing and fermentation temperatures. Brewing methods were still archaic. In a letter to Joseph Brooks in London, Wilson wrote, 'Every part of the business is done by hand-pail, from drawing of the mash to filling the casks for exportation. It occurs to me that this quantity of business could be done with the aid of machinery to some great expense, and with equal certainty of purpose.' Country brewing lagged far behind the big porter brewers in London, where Samuel Whitbread had installed a steam engine, built by James Watt, in 1785 to provide power for the brewing processes. And the Burton brewers were still comparatively small. As late as 1830, most of the brewers in the town were producing around 3,000 barrels a year each. The years of massive production lay ahead.

Bass steam-powered wagon in the National Brewery Centre.

Burton brewing may have been small compared to London's, but a further letter of Wilson's in 1791 showed he was aware of changes in the appreciation of beer in the south of the country. He told a customer in the Baltic: 'I have committed one fault in the brewing of my ale last winter, and that is, in making it too strong – if I had made it weaker it certainly would have been lighter coloured and would have pleased better at first sight; but it is certainly better for the interest of the adventure to possess strength sufficient for its certain conservation, than to be otherwise and in danger of turning sour.' In London, porter, a dark beer of which the strongest version was known as stout porter or stout for short, was the drink of the working class. Wealthy entrepreneurs and aristocrats, along with the first stirrings of a white-collar middle class, wanted a more refined and therefore paler beer. In common with Marie Antoinette, they felt that dark bread and beer should be left to the hoi-polloi. But the strength of Burton ale, as Wilson indicated, was a bar to making paler beer. Steve Wellington, who brewed with Bass for many years and who now runs the William Worthington craft brewery within the National Brewery Centre in Burton, stills brews Bass No. 1, which, at 10.5 per cent alcohol, is a true Old Burton Ale, even though it's labelled a barley wine today. As a result of the strength of the beer, it requires an enormously long, twelve-hour boil in the copper with hops, compared with one or two hours for the average beer. No. 1 is made only with pale malt, but during the boil some of the malt sugars are 'caramelised' and the result is a dark amber ale. In the eighteenth century, most brewers, the porter brewers in particular, were still using brown malt, but pale malt

Stacks of casks formed 'pyramids'.

was beginning to become more available and would transform brewing in the following century. (See the end of the chapter for an explanation of malting.)

Wilson Junior produced no children. He took his nephew Samuel Allsopp into the business and, in 1807, following a downturn in trade, Wilson sold the brewery to Allsopp for £7,000. Samuel Allsopp was succeeded by his sons Charles and Henry and the name Wilson, so critical to the growth of brewing in the town, disappeared when the company was renamed Samuel Allsopp & Sons in 1822. The Allsopps were unusual brewers. Most of their competitors came from artisan backgrounds but the Allsopps were an ancient and aristocratic English family. Hugh de Allsopp (spelt either Alsop or Alsup at the time) went with Richard I to fight in the Holy Land in the twelfth century and was knighted at the siege of Acre. He was awarded substantial lands in Derbyshire by a grateful monarch. The reason why his descendants became involved in much-despised 'trade' was the result of the feudal system of primogeniture, in which land and titles passed to the eldest son. Other children were well-educated but were given no money. In the case of the Allsopps, many entered the church and the army or became farmers and craftsmen. This accounts for members of the family in the late eighteenth century becoming brewers.

The downturn in trade at the start of the nineteenth century was the result of Britain's escalating problems with Napoleon's France, which was to have a devastating impact in Burton. Wilson and then Allsopp faced a new domestic challenge from a relative latecomer to brewing in the town: William Bass.

Bass was born in Hinckley, Leicestershire, around 1717 – the date is not precise. His parents were John and Ann Bass; John was a plumber and glazier and he must have prospered as he bought a large house and smallholding in 1725 in Castle End, Hinckley. John and Ann had three sons, John, William and Thomas, and the income from both the father's work and the smallholding allowed the family to lead a comfortable life. The smallholding included a small brew house where Ann, in the manner of a medieval brewster, made ale. William was introduced to brewing at an early stage of his life and may have helped his mother make ale. He would certainly have been well aware of the way in which beer was made.

The family's life changed dramatically in 1732 when the father died suddenly at the age of just forty-four years. William, who was fifteen at the time, was put in charge of the smallholding while his brother John carried on the plumbing and glazing business and also began to deliver cider to inns and houses in the villages of Leicestershire and Warwickshire. John was a respected member of the community, several times serving as a constable, but William ran in to trouble on a number of occasions and was fined for 'killing, selling or exposing corrupt flesh' – presumably the corrupt flesh was of the animal rather than the human variety. In spite of his youthful indiscretions, William's work flourished. He travelled to Birmingham to collect cider as well as malt, hops, bottles and corks for his mother's brew house. The cider side of the business expanded, with innkeepers in Oakham, Stamford and Uppingham demanding regular supplies. In 1751, William formerly went into partnership with his brother John, and the following year they created a carrying company that operated between Manchester and London. The Bass family claimed for many years that William was able to set up the carrying business as a result of winning the substantial sum of £500 in a lottery while he was working as a porter in London. What is not in dispute is that the carrying business dominated William's life for more than twenty years. In 1775, he took complete control of the company when his brother John decided to concentrate on plumbing and glazing in Hinckley. William, on the other hand, travelled widely. While he was in London he met his future wife, Mary Gibbons, the daughter of Michael Gibbons, the landlord of the Red Lion in Gray's Inn Lane. The pub was close to the Inns of Court and attracted a wealthy clientele of lawyers and judges. Gibbons brewed on the premises and William Bass noted for future use the manner in which the well-to-do customers of the inn enjoyed their ale. When Gibbons died, he left Mary £420 and half his estate. She married William Bass, probably in 1756, and they set up in some style in Nether Hall, Wetmore, on the outskirts of Burton. He chose the area as he was doing good business in Burton, carrying locally made hats, hardware and beer to London and Manchester.

William made a handsome living from his carrying business yet, at the age of sixty, rather than retiring, he decided to enter the brewing industry. He was prompted by the fact that, increasingly, his wagons were taking ale to London from Burton brewers. But he also saw that the development of river and canal traffic in the Midlands would eventually eclipse road transport and he was determined to provide a secure future for his sons Michael and William. He observed the success – and the profits – being made by Burton brewers, Wilson in particular, from the trade with Russia and the Baltic and he wanted a share.

In 1767, William paved the way for his entry in to brewing by selling some of his wagons to Samuel Sadler. In 1777, he sold the remainder of the business to the major firm of Pickford when he moved into premises in Burton's High Street, though he kept some wagons and horses to avoid paying carrying costs. He paid £1,050 for the freehold of land and buildings that occupied one acre and included a 'dwelling house' described as 'well-built and commodious... containing a spacious hall, five large parlours, bed chamber, butler's pantry etc on the lower floor; Bed chamber on the 2nd floor; attic storey. Stable for 8 horses, brew-house, pigeon-house, coach-house etc, walled garden with fishponds'. The buildings, empty for two years, had been used for brewing by Thomas James and William Yeomans, and they provided William with a simple entry into the trade without the need to build a brewery from scratch. He was made well aware of the intense competition he faced as his brewery stood between the plants of Benjamin Wilson and William Worthington and opposite those of Henry Evans and John Walker Wilson.

Undaunted, William set out from this modest little brewery to build his new business. The contacts he'd made during his carrying years held him in good stead. By 1782, he was not only supplying local merchants and innkeepers with beer in Burton and Derby but was also selling to outlets in London and Manchester. In London he supplied the Coffee House in Cheapside, Mrs Mills' Peahen in Gray's Inn Road, the Fox & Goose in Highgate and the Great Turnstile in Holborn. They bought Bass beer for 18*d* to 24*d* a gallon, considerably more than they paid for London beer, porter in particular. But they had wealthy clients who were prepared to pay a high price for Burton ale.

Once he had established a successful trade in England, William set out to tackle the lucrative Baltic market. Between 1782 and 1783 he appointed agents in Danzig and St Petersburg. His records show that in March 1785 he sent forty hogsheads (a hogshead holds 54 imperial gallons) and ninety half-hogsheads to Hull for shipping to Danzig. For both the domestic and foreign markets, William was aware of the need to brew the highest quality ale. At first he bought most of his barley from Newark but he soon looked further afield to Norfolk, a county that was emerging as the supplier of the best malting barley. While the London porter brewers were content to buy brown malt from Hertfordshire, the Burton brewers were keenly aware of the need to make their ales lighter in colour and to use predominantly pale malt. Towards the end of the eighteenth century, Bass and

Michael Bass, the Burton entrepreneur who rapidly expanded the company.

the other Burton brewers were starting to buy coke from smelters in Derby as the fuel for their malt kilns. Hops were bought from Kent, even though the plants were more easily available from both Herefordshire and Worcestershire, but again William was determined to buy the best.

William Bass's brewing career was brief. His wife Mary died in 1786 and William followed the following year. But in just ten years he had succeeded in building a small but profitable brewing business, which he left to his son Michael (the other son, William, was not interested in brewing). Michael had one overriding ambition: to overtake Benjamin Wilson as the major brewer in Burton. That was a considerable challenge, for in 1790 Wilson merged with Sketchley's brewery and increased capacity to 4,500 barrels a year. Michael Bass responded the following year by joining forces with James Musgrave, who ran the oldest brewery in the town, one which had been founded by Printon. Musgrave supplied Michael Bass with many new customers in London and Manchester and also helped expand the Baltic side of the business. By the end of the century, Bass was brewing some 3,500 barrels of beer a year, of which around 30 per cent was exported. Bass was less reliant on the export trade than Wilson, an important consideration as Britain's relationship with France deteriorated. From 1792, Hull trawlers had to sail in convoy to avoid attack from Bonaparte's fleet and convoy costs and higher insurances rates hit brewers' profitability. Michael Bass was nevertheless determined to drive on into Europe and the Baltic and by the turn of the century he had nine agents in St Petersburg, eleven in Riga, twenty-five in Danzig, one in Elsinore and four each in Bremen, Hamburg and Hanover. The relationship with Musgrave was brief and the partnership was dissolved by mutual agreement in 1797. Michael Bass must have been a difficult man to work with. Unknown to Musgrave, he turned his commercial traveller John Ratcliff into a partner, though this was not formalised until 1809, when the company became Bass & Ratcliff. In 1797, the two partners built and opened a new brew house in the High Street. Michael could be unscrupulous as well as difficult. He was twice asked by agents in Danzig to brand his casks 'B. Wilson' as a result of Wilson's greater standing in Europe, and Michael 'reluctantly' agreed to this subterfuge.

As a result of the uncertainty in the Baltic, the Burton brewers looked for new markets both at home and abroad. They faced fresh competition from Thomas Salt. Salt had been a leading maltster in the town but at the turn of the century he bought Clay's brewery and quickly turned his company into one of the leading brewers in Burton. Determined to maintain their dominance, Bass and Wilson attacked the trade in Lancashire, increased their sales in London and the south and even sold English ale to Scotland. They found agents who would take their beer in the Caribbean, North America and then to Australia – a mighty journey by sailing ship. In 1798, a Captain Raven reported to a relieved Michael Bass that ale shipped to New South Wales had arrived in excellent condition and 'was considered a most suitable commodity for export'.

The new markets were vital as exports to the Baltic became increasingly hazardous and less profitable. In 1783, tariffs on British goods imported through St Petersburg increased by 300 per cent. Trade to Russia ceased completely in 1800, when Russia placed an embargo on all British ships and merchandise. The Burton brewers turned their attention to Prussia and Poland, and at first sales were brisk. But the entire trade in the Baltic and central and eastern Europe collapsed as Bonaparte's armies and navy closed port after port to the British. The impact in Burton was nothing less than catastrophic. Between 1780 and the mid-1820s, the number of breweries in the town fell from thirteen to just five: Bass & Ratcliff, Allsopp (formerly Wilson), Worthington, John Sherratt and Salt. In Horninglow, still a separate village outside the town, John Marston ran a small brewery that had started as Coats & Co around 1800. The desperate search for new internal markets can been in the activities of Samuel Allsopp. Instead of exporting his beer from Liverpool, he now looked to sell it in the pubs of the great sea port but the costs of transport by canal made his beer expensive. He complained in a letter to Arthur Heywood in Liverpool, 'If we lived only a few miles nearer, we could sell our Malt Liquor upon the same terms as the Liverpool Brewers do and would soon acquire a fortune'. Allsopp arranged for contacts in the Midlands and the north to act as his agents and every letter he sent to his clients begged them to recommend his ale to their friends. Writing to James Culmer in Canterbury, he said plaintively, 'We have no connections in your part of the country, not having been engaged in the country business long'. He offered free samples of beer to publicans in London and opened a warehouse with a manager in Eastcheap in order to improve sales in the capital. But the manager, Robert Oates, pocketed part of the proceeds and had to be dismissed. Allsopp closed the warehouse in disgust and used agents on commission instead.

As the industrial revolution gathered pace, new technology came to the aid of the beleaguered brewers. In the 1790s, they began to use attemperators, devices already widely used by distillers to control the temperature of the mash and fermentation. Attemperators, known colloquially as 'worms', were lengths of coiled copper piping through which cool water circulated. The device was placed in mash tuns to control the heat of malt and 'liquor' (brewing water) and the same device was put into fermenting vessels to maintain an even temperature. The worm could be used in reverse, with warm water used in winter if temperatures fell so low that fermentation could not get under way. Suddenly, it was possible for brewers to extend the brewing season and their problems were further eased later in the nineteenth century with the arrival of ice-making machines and refrigerators. At the same time, the rapid development of the coke industry in the late eighteenth and early nineteenth centuries meant that pale malt became available in abundance, enabling the brewers to lighten the colour of their beer.

Allsopp took the lead in improving Burton ale for the domestic market. He had learnt from his efforts to sell beer in London and the Home Counties that he needed to make his beer lighter in colour. He wrote to customers asking 'whether Pale Ale or that of a darker Colour is most liked with you'. He asked his London agent to send him a 'bottle of the Windsor ale – in a Box safe and say how much it is sold pr. Barell' so he could model his beer on it. (Windsor Ale was made with pale malt with the addition of honey.) Allsopp also recognised the need to make his beer more bitter: drinkers in both Liverpool and London were demanding beers with greater hop character. This move to pale, bitter beers in Burton was to pave the way for a dramatic change in beer style that would enrich the brewers in the nineteenth century as they found a new overseas market for their ales.

Barley and malt

Brewers call barley 'the soul of beer'. Other grains, such as oats, rice, rye and wheat, can be used in the production of beer but barley is the preferred grain as it delivers a rich, biscuit flavour and works in harmony with yeast. It's a tough grain with a husk that acts as a natural filter during the initial mashing stage: other grains without a husk can become 'gummy' and block brewing vessels.

Before beer can be made, barley has to be turned into malt. Malting triggers a natural chemical process that begins to turn starch into sugar. The type of sugar that results is maltose and is highly fermentable. For centuries, grain was taken from surrounding fields when brewing was a domestic affair, produced in abbeys, inns and people's homes. But as commercial brewing developed, brewers searched for the best grain to ensure consistency of quality and to avoid waste that would affect their profits. Over time, Bedfordshire, Cambridgeshire, Hertfordshire, Lincolnshire, Norfolk and Suffolk were found to be the best producers of barley fit for brewing as a result of the light, well-drained soil in these counties. The result was thin-skinned, plump barley, ideal for malting. In the eighteenth century, the powerful porter brewers in London took the bulk of their malt supplies from Hertfordshire, where the town of Ware, in particular, produced high-quality brown malt that was shipped to London via the River Lea. Brown malt was 'kilned' – dried and roasted – in a kiln fuelled by wood, usually hornbeam. Dark malt was needed by the porter brewers to give their beer the required colour along with a nutty and slightly scorched flavour demanded by drinkers.

The Burton brewers in the eighteenth and nineteenth centuries preferred to use pale malt as they sought to lighten the colour of their beers. Pale malt is more gently heated than brown malt and retains a higher level of the enzymes that turn starch into sugar. This means less malt is needed to produce beer – an important cost consideration. But pale malt needs a different fuel in the kiln – wood is hard to control and it can flare, producing a scorched or charred end product. Early in the eighteenth century, Abraham Darby started to turn coal from the Staffordshire mines into coke – coal without the natural gases – and the result was a new type of fuel that was seized on by the nearby Burton brewers: Benjamin Wilson's record books refer to buying 'coaks' from Derby. Coke was much easier to control and gave off consistent heat. Coal had been used to make pale malt in country areas but it was not a satisfactory fuel as a result of the gases created when it was burnt, which infected the malt with off-flavours. As the industrial revolution gathered pace and coke was made on a large scale, the Burton brewers had the ideal fuel for their maltings. Eventually, even the London porter brewers switched to pale malt, blending in darker malts for the necessary colour.

To make malt, barley is taken from the fields to maltings where it's washed or 'steeped' in water to clean it. The grain absorbs the water, which encourages germination. The grain is next spread on heated floors or placed in rotating drums for germination to take place: craft brewers believe that 'floor malted barley' makes the finest beer. Biochemical changes take place inside the grain as it germinates: the starch becomes soluble as rootlets break through the husk. Hidden from sight, the plant's embryo, the main root or acrospire, starts to grow, triggering a change that turns proteins into enzymes that will convert soluble starch into sugar during the mashing stage in the brewery. Only partial germination takes places in the maltings: final germination occurs in the brewery.

When the maltster is satisfied that germination has progressed to the right stage, the grain is transferred to a kiln, a type of oven where the grain is spread over a perforated metal floor. Heat comes up from below; the fuel used today is gas. For pale malt, the temperature rises from 65 to 75 degrees Celsius, increasing to 90 degrees for the final eight hours. Higher temperatures are needed to make darker malts such as amber, brown, black and chocolate.

Burton Ale – the Legacy

There's ale from Burton and then there's Burton Ale. A distinctive style of beer from the town started to develop in the eighteenth century. Before then we can only hazard a guess at what the ales brewed by monks and tavern keepers were like. They almost certainly augmented barley malt with other grains from local fields. Herbs and plants would have been used for bitterness before the arrival of the hop in the fifteenth century. From the eighteenth century, as the influence of Allsopps, Bass, Worthington and other commercial brewers grew, Burton Ale became a recognised style, one that was prized in both London and St Petersburg. The history of Burton Ale falls into two categories. There was the strong, nut brown beer brewed primarily for the export trade, followed by lighter, amber-coloured ale for the domestic market. In spite of the success of pale ale and India Pale Ale in the nineteenth century, Burton Ale remained a popular beer in the twentieth century and survives today under a variety of names. During the Second World

The 'beerage' meets the monarchy: Edward VII, centre foreground, at Lord Burton's estate in 1902. Lord Burton is third from the right, back row. (*See* page 91)

War, the beer took on a macabre note when British pilots would say, if one of their colleagues was shot down over the English Channel, 'He's gone for a Burton'.

The version that I'll call Old Burton, the style brewed for export, would at first have been brewed using brown malt but, as the eighteenth century developed, brewers would have switched to pale malt cured over coke fires. As explained above, these strong beers, ranging from 10.5 per cent to 12 per cent, were dark in colour, even though they were brewed with pale malt, as a result of a long boil with hops that 'caramelised' some of the brewing sugar. The style exists today in the shape of Bass No. 1, now produced in the William Worthington Brewery in Burton. The beer is called barley wine today, a term that masks the historic importance of the style. Bass No. 1, which was also the base for King's Ale, brewed to commemorate the coronation of Edward VII in 1902, is 10.5 per cent and was originally made with pale malt and Fuggles and Goldings hops.

The Durden Park Beer Circle, a group of passionate home brewers dedicated to reproducing old beer styles, lists – in its booklet, *Old British Beers and How to Make Them* – a recipe for a Burton Ale from 1824 that has an original gravity of 1,140 degrees, approximately 11.5 per cent in modern terms. It was brewed with pale malt and unspecified hops, and was matured in cask for one and a half years. In Scotland, Younger's brewery in Edinburgh in 1872 brewed an export beer of the Old Burton style with a gravity of 1,120, brewed with pale malt and Goldings hops and which was matured for 'at least a year'. Younger's ledgers show that the company obtained malt not only from England and Scotland but also from Ireland, France, the Baltic, the Black Sea area, North Africa and, occasionally, from the United States.

The impact of paler Burton Ales for the domestic market was so profound that just about every brewery in the country found it necessary to have 'a Burton' in its portfolio. A nineteenth-century price list in the now closed Young's brewery in Wandsworth, south London, included a Burton and it survives today as Young's Winter Warmer, brewed by Wells & Young's in Bedford. The beer is 5.5 per cent and is brewed with Maris Otter pale ale malt, crystal malt and brewing sugar, with Fuggles and Goldings hops. In Chiswick, west London, Fuller's multi-award-winning ESB (Extra Special Bitter), also 5.5 per cent, developed from the company's former Burton. In January 2011, Fuller's launched the first in a series of Past Masters, beers based on nineteenth-century recipes. It will include a Burton Ale from that period and it will be interesting to see how it differs from ESB.

In 1891, when the Suffolk brewer Sir Edward Greene died following fifty-five years in the business, the *London Star* newspaper said in an obituary, 'He was one of the first country brewers to discover that beer need not be a vile, black turgid stuff, but brewed a bright amber-coloured liquid of the Burton type which he sold at 1s a gallon and made a fortune.' It's possible that Greene King's popular strong bitter, Abbot Ale (5 per cent), is descended from the 'Burton type' of the nineteenth century. It's brewed with pale ale malt, coloured malt, brewing sugar and caramel, and hopped with English varieties.

A beer called Draught Burton Ale should offer the closest link to the town's style. The beer was first called Ind Coope Draught Burton Ale and was brewed in the Allsopp's plant in 1976, when the Allied Breweries group was anxious to jump on the real ale bandwagon created by the Campaign for Real Ale. DBA, as it was known for short, was a cask-conditioned version of the group's best-selling bottled pale ale Double Diamond. DBA was a great success but, when Allied Breweries broke up, the new owners of the group's beers, Carlsberg, switched production to its Tetley's plant in Leeds and seemed to lose interest in it. Tetley's was due to close in 2011 and DBA is currently brewed for Carlsberg by J. W. Lees in Manchester. It's now extremely difficult to find but is worth seeking out. The recipe given to me in 1993 by Ind Coope was sparse on detail:

Original Gravity 1,047 degrees. Alcohol by volume, 4.8 per cent.
Ingredients: pale malt, chocolate malt, liquid sugar. UK bittering hops with Styrian Goldings for aroma and dry hopping.

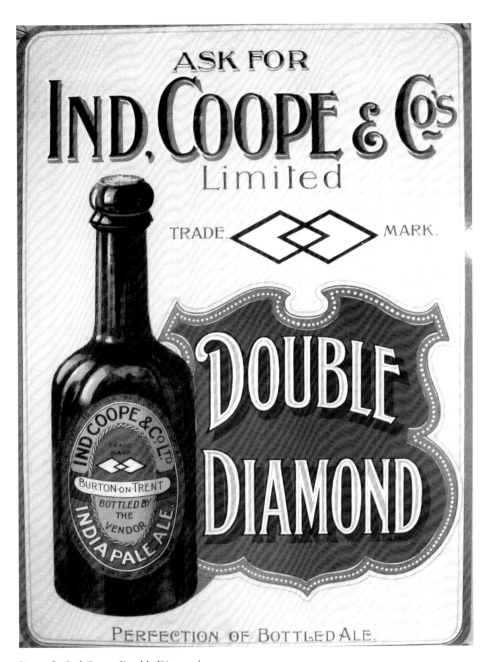

Poster for Ind Coope Double Diamond.

My tasting note in my book the *Real Ale Almanac* said:

Nose: stunning aromas of malt, rich hops and marmalade fruit.
Palate: massive, mouth-filling balance of malt and hops with a long finish full of hops and fruit notes.
Comments: Magnificent powerful ale; casks are heavily primed with sugar for secondary fermentation and the ABV can reach 5.1 per cent or 5.2 per cent.

'Dry hopping' means that a small amount of hops is added to each cask of beer when it leaves the brewery for additional aroma and flavour. Styrian Goldings (now known as Bobek) are grown in Slovenia and are mainly used in lager brewing, but many British brewers also use them for their fine floral and spicy aroma.

I suspect DBA was a hybrid beer, a cross between a true Burton Ale and the pale ales that followed in the nineteenth century. The 'new' Burton Ale developed by Allsopps used – as far as is known – just pale malt. Brewing sugar, as we shall see later, was used when the Burton brewers started to produce India Pale Ale. Heavily roasted malts such as chocolate became available in 1817 when Daniel Wheeler invented a roasting machine similar to a coffee roaster. The dark malts produced by this method were seized on by the London porter brewers, but their use would have been negligible in Burton. DBA may not be strictly a true Burton Ale but its origins lie in the town, and it is a delicious beer.

Bruce Wilkinson, who runs the Burton Bridge Brewery in the town with his partner Geoff Mumford, worked for Ind Coope and brewed DBA. He says his Bridge Bitter (OG 1042, ABV 4.2 per cent) is his interpretation of a Burton Ale. The recipe is: Pipkin pale malt (95 per cent), crystal malt (5 per cent); Challenger (67 per cent) and Target (33 per cent) whole hops in the copper; dry hopped with Styrian Goldings. My tasting note in the *Real Ale Almanac* is as follows:

Nose: vinous aroma with powerful hop notes.
Palate: rich fruit and malt in the mouth with deep, dry finish packed with sultana notes.
Comments: complex golden beer, winey and hoppy.

Chapter Four

TO INDIA AND BACK

In 1822, the chairman of the East India Co., Campbell Marjoribanks, invited Samuel Allsopp to dinner in his London mansion in Upper Wimpole Street. Marjoribanks, whose name was pronounced Marchbanks, was a wealthy trader with India. He made three voyages there between 1795 and 1807 and, as a result, he was invited to join the 'court of directors' of the East India Co. He later became EIC chairman, serving three terms in that post. He was therefore a powerful and influential figure in a company founded by royal charter in 1600 by Elizabeth I and which had grown to exercise almost monopoly control over trade with the Indian sub-continent. The monopoly was relaxed in 1813, allowing independent entrepreneurs such as ships' commanders to capture part of the India trade.

Marjoribanks had a problem with a London brewer named Hodgson. He knew, too, that Allsopp had a far bigger problem: the loss of his entire trade with Russia and the Baltic. The chairman of the East India Co. had a scheme that he thought could be mutually beneficial. Over dinner, Allsopp bewailed his fate: he had lost his export trade, his business was floundering and Burton was in crisis. Marjoribanks responded by telling him to forget the Baltic and attack the Indian trade instead. 'India,' the chairman of the EIC told Allsopp, offered 'a trade that can never be lost: for the climate is too hot for brewing. We are now dependant on Hodgson who has given offence to most of the merchants of India. But your Burton ale, so strong and sweet, will not suit our market.'

It's possible to report the conversation because Allsopp later recounted it to a Burton journalist and it was recorded in a book, *Burton and its Bitter Beer,* by John Stevenson Bushnan in 1853. Warming to his theme, Marjoribanks added a rider that had special appeal to Allsopp: Britain's dominion over India meant

India Pale Ale in hold of ship en route to India. Note the staves at ends of barrels to stop them exploding during the voyage. (Model at National Brewery Centre, Burton.)

that brewers who sold beer there would not face tariffs of any kind. The EIC chairman's butler, with the deft skills of his calling, appeared on cue with a bottle of Hodgson's ale, which he poured for the two diners. Allsopp was intrigued by the beer and he said he would take a bottle back to Burton to ask his brewers for their advice. Most importantly, the message from Marjoribanks reinforced what Allsopp himself had known for some time: he had to make a paler, more bitter beer if his business were to recover.

The route to India for the Burton brewers was charted for them by a comparatively small brewer in East London, Abbot & Hodgson of Bromley-by-Bow, founded in 1752. George Hodgson was the early driving force behind the brewery and he had the good fortune to make beer in a part of London that was close to the East India Docks. Abbot & Hodgson, on the banks of the River Lea, was ideally placed for delivering beer by barge to the docks at Blackwall. Seventy ships supplied the East India trade, and Hodgson learned from drinking with sailors in a docklands pub called the Bombay Grab – named after an Indian dhow – that the costs of sending goods to India were comparatively low, as ships left half empty: the holds filled up with exotic silks and spices on the return trips. Hodgson was urged by the captains of the ships, who were keen to profit from the business, to export beer to India.

He was already brewing porter and his company continued to send dark beer to India until the 1820s. But, in common with Allsopp, he was encouraged to produce a paler and hoppier beer that would appeal to the rapidly growing number of civil servants, clerks, army personnel and the gentry of the Raj who were stationed in India, and who needed a refreshing beer in that torrid climate. It's unlikely that Hodgson developed or even 'invented' a beer called India Pale Ale. It was difficult at that time to brew a pale beer in London. The well waters available from the Thames Valley, below clay beds, are rich in calcium carbonate that draws out the saccharine character of malt and is best suited to producing dark beer such as porter. The major London brewer, Barclay Perkins, for example, struggled to make an acceptable pale beer.

The brewing historian Martyn Cornell, in his book *Beer: the Story of the Pint*, argues that Hodgson adapted a style known as October Beer for the India trade. This was a beer produced, as the name suggests, in the autumn when temperatures permitted brewing to re-start following the summer. It was country ale brewed for the gentry. In the late eighteenth century, as London became a fashionable place to live, the gentry moved to the capital and brought with them their taste and demand for October Beer. While the London porter brewers remained faithful to brown, wood-cured malt, October Beer was brewed with paler malt cured over coke fires. It was powerful ale of around 1,140 degrees gravity or more, or 11.5 per cent alcohol. During the interminable wars with France, patriotic English gentlemen and women refused to touch imported French wine and drank strong beer that matched claret or Burgundy in strength instead. Cornell records that a brewer named George Watkins, who worked in the 1760s, said October Beer 'would be ready for bottling after twelve months, and should be kept in bottle for a further year, making it two years old before it was fit to drink'.

This was the ideal beer to survive the rigors of a long sea journey to India that took ships some three or more months to sail along the coast of Africa, round the Cape and up through the Indian Ocean to Bombay and Calcutta. As a result of the beer's strength and the large amount of hops used, the beer in its oak casks, protected by alcohol, hops and yeast, arrived in fine drinking form in spite of often tumultuous seas and considerable variations in temperature. From 1784, the *Calcutta Gazette* carried advertisements for 'London pale ale' and in January 1801 the paper announced the arrival of 'beer from Hodgson... just landed and now exposed for sale for ready money only'. The style of beer was underscored in 1822 when the *Gazette* reported that goods landed from London included 'Hodgson's warranted prime picked ale of the genuine October brewing'.

In 1811, George Hodgson was succeeded by his son Mark, who energetically expanded the export of beer. By 1813 he was shipping some 4,000 barrels a year to India, four times the amount sent in 1801. In 1821, the brewery, now run by

Frederick Hodgson and Thomas Drane, was rebuilt and expanded at Bow Bridge. Hodgson and Drane took a momentous decision that would lead ultimately to their eclipse: they decided to cut out both the East India Co. and captains of independent ships, transport their beer direct and retail it in India themselves. They registered as shippers in the City of London. In India, they refused all credit, would only accept cash – they had previously given employees of the EIC twelve or eighteen months' credit – and raised their prices by 20 per cent. The greed shown by Hodgson and Drane outraged everyone connected with trade to India: ships' captains who had made a tidy profit – as high as £12,000 a year – from carrying the brewery's beer, merchants in India, and the mighty East India Co. It was a serious error to annoy the EIC. It led to Campbell Marjoribanks inviting Samuel Allsopp to dinner and, as a result, the brewer took samples of Hodgson's beer back to Burton.

Job Goodhead was head brewer at Allsopps. When he tasted Hodgson's beer, he spat it out in disgust, affronted by its extreme bitterness, but he said he could kiln his malt to make a beer as light in colour. According to a local story, Goodhead made a trial brew in a tea pot; why did he use a tea pot when he had a brewery at his fingertips, including small vessels set aside for short-run beers such as porter and stout? It seems an odd thing to do, but it has gone down in Burton folklore. Allsopp soon had a batch of beer ready for India. In a small town such as Burton, where brewery workers congregated in ale houses after work, reports of the new style of beer spread like a bush fire and Bass and Thomas Salt were soon experimenting with their own ales for India. They were taking a considerable risk. They had to invest in large casks – hogsheads and butts – with staves cut twice as thick as those used for the domestic market to prevent them exploding as the beer continued to ferment on the long voyages. Unlike Hodgson, they had to pay transport costs to get the beer to the London or Liverpool docks before meeting the additional costs of shipping to India. They had to supply bottles and corks in order that casks could be broken down on arrival and decanted into bottles for domestic use. And when their ales reached their destination, they had to pass muster with tasters who could accept or reject a whole consignment. Allsopp heard to his horror that his first consignment, while accepted by the tasters, earned only twenty rupees a hogshead, while Hodgson's rated twenty-five. But the second and third consignments brought forty rupees per hogshead each and Allsopp never looked back. A letter from a J.C. Bailton gave Allsopp great heart:

> With reference to the loss you have sustained in your first shipments, you must have been prepared for that, had you known the market as well as I do: Here almost everything is name, and Hodgson's has so long stood without a rival that it was a matter of astonishment how your ale could have stood the competition;

but that it did is a fact, and I myself was present when a butt of yours reached 136 rupees, and a butt of Hodgson's only eighty rupees at a public sale.

The rapid success of Allsopp's beer in India was due not only to the skill of Job Goodhead and his brewing staff but also to Burton water. The mineral-rich well waters now came in to their own, bringing out the full flavours of malt and hops in the new pale beer. The quality of Burton-brewed pale ale was confirmed by the major Bristol porter brewery, George's, which attempted to enter the India trade. In 1828 a senior partner at George's wrote to Willis & Earle in Calcutta suggesting it would not be difficult to improve on Hodgson's beer: 'We neither like its thick and muddy appearance or rank bitter flavour'. Twenty months later George's shipped twenty hogsheads to India and the same writer noted: 'We made a slight alteration in the Ale by brewing it rather of a paler colour and more hop'd to make it as similar as possible to some samples of Allsopp's ale'. Allsopp had improved on Hodgson's beer in every way: it was paler, hoppier and arrived in India in better condition.

Burton was about to take off. When Peel's cotton mills collapsed in 1841 – ironically as a result of cheap imports from India – brewing became the major industry in the town. Peter Mathias, the official historian of the industry, says in *The Brewing Industry in England 1700-1830*, 'Burton-on-Trent remained the only true example in the British Isles of a "brewing town" in the same economically significant sense that Dundee was a jute town or Merthyr Tydfil an iron town'. The point is well made, because Burton was not an oddity that happened to make beer but was at the heart, socially and economically, of a surging, confident, unprecedented new form of production. The social historian Eric Hobsbawm says, in *Industry and Empire*:

The Industrial Revolution marks the most fundamental transformation of human life in the history of the world recorded in written documents. For a brief period it coincided with the history of a single country, Great Britain. An entire world economy was thus built on, or rather around, Britain, and this country therefore temporarily rose to a position of global influence and power unparalleled by any state of its relative size before or since, and unlikely to be paralleled by any state in the foreseeable future. There was a moment in the world's history when Britain can be described, if we are not too pedantic, as its only workshop, its only massive importer and exporter, its only carrier, its only imperialist, almost its only foreign investor.

Benjamin Wilson, who bemoaned the outdated technology available to him in the 1790s, would have been astonished by the changes in Burton a few decades later. Cast-iron mash tuns held heat better than wood, were far larger, holding up to

200,000 gallons of the sugary extract called wort, and had longer life spans. Mashing was made more effective and the temperature of grain and water maintained by 'pre-mashing' devices based on the Archimedes screw principle. Steam-driven rakes stirred the mash, releasing horses from the drudgery of plodding endlessly round mash tuns to turn the rakes. In the middle of the nineteenth century, Scottish brewers developed a system known as sparging that enabled the grain in the mash tun to be sprinkled with hot brewing liquor by rotating arms in the roof of the vessel. The method washed out any remaining malt sugars and put paid to the old system of producing three or more beers of decreasing strength from the same mash. As a result, mash tuns could be utilised more effectively by pushing through new brews every few hours.

Coppers, fired by coal or coke, were turned from open pans into enclosed domed vessels that avoided heat loss and retained the essential aromas of the hops. Large open pans, where the hopped wort cooled prior to fermentation, were replaced by heat exchange units: the wort was pumped through pipes or plates that alternated with pipes holding running cold water. The wort was no longer open to the atmosphere and as a result was free from the risk of infection from wild yeasts and bacteria. When ice-making machines were invented, they were embraced with as much enthusiasm in Burton as they were by lager brewers in Bavaria. The 'Burton Union' system of fermentation, introduced in 1838, produced a cleaner fermentation that resulted in a sparkling and clear glass of ale that appealed to discerning drinkers. Louis Pasteur's work on yeast towards the end of the century encouraged brewers to build laboratories and install microscopes in order to isolate pure strains and avoid infections. Well-prepared pale malt delivered higher levels of fermentable sugar than wood-cured brown malt. The result was better-quality beer made more cheaply, an important consideration for brewers anxious to maximise their profits.

In short, brewing in Burton was no longer a slow, labour-intensive, artisanal craft that took place only between the months of October and April. It was an industry based on year-round mass production, using all the skills and machinery unleashed by the Industrial Revolution. Within a few decades, not only brewing but the town itself had been transformed. By 1861, the population was three times as high as in 1801 and it then doubled by 1878, when Burton became a municipal borough. The figure doubled again to 50,000 by 1901 when the town was given the status of a county borough. In 1851, the breweries employed around a third of the male working population, rising to half by the late 1880s.

Driven by the quest for new markets to replace the lost Baltic trade, and aided by new technology, the brewers, Allsopp and Bass in particular, set out to dominate the export of pale ale to India. (It should be noted in passing that the term India Pale Ale was not used by all brewers. Hodgson's beer was called India

Ale and all imports from England were usually described simply as pale ale in the sub-continent. Bass never used the term, preferring to call its beer Burton Pale Ale. Other brewers, more pedantically, called their export beers East India Pale Ale.) To the chagrin of Samuel Allsopp, Bass became both the major brewer and major exporter in Burton. In the years 1832 and 1833, of 12,000 barrels of beer reaching Bengal, Bass accounted for 5,200, Allsopp 1,400 and Hodgson 3,600. Within a decade Allsopp and Bass accounted for more than half the beer shipped to Calcutta. Hodgson's dropped their prices in a desperate attempt to win back market share but the superior quality of the Burton beers saw them off. The London firm went into decline and was eventually put up for sale in 1855. It was bought by Smith, Garrett & Co. and the Bow brewery survived until 1927, when it was taken over the leading London brewer Taylor Walker, based nearby at the Barley Mow Brewery in Limehouse. The Hodgson site closed in 1933 and is now occupied by former London County Council flats named Prioress House.

Exports from Burton increased at a rate of nautical knots. In 1840, some 20,000 barrels of ale were exported to India and the business rose to a peak of 217,000 barrels by 1870. Allsopps said the production of pale ale was its 'first consideration' as new markets opened up. The Australian gold rush in the 1850s sent 400,000 British emigrants Down Under in search of wealth — and pale ale followed them. More modern clipper ships could make the journey in sixty-eight days. In Scotland, the Edinburgh brewers had discovered that the spring waters from the 'Charmed Circle' beneath the city centre were mineral-rich in common with Burton's and enabled them to switch to pale ale production. Younger of Edinburgh exported to Australia, New Zealand and to the United States. Its pale ale was so popular in New York City that a brewer in the suburbs attempted to pass off a beer with a label almost identical to Younger's called Yonkers Pale Ale. The Burton brewers were also busy in the American market. Bass's Ale, as it was called there, was listed on the menu of the dining cars of the Union Pacific transcontinental railroad, while Allsopp's pale ale won prizes in the Centennial Brewers' Exhibition in Philadelphia in 1876.

The peak figure of exports in 1870 is significant, for India Pale Ale went into rapid decline after that. The success of the beer contained the seeds of its downfall. In the 1820s and '30s, Anton Dreher and Gabriel Sedlmayr the Younger made extensive tours of major brewing countries in order to help them perfect their own products. Dreher owned a brewery in Vienna while Sedlmayr ran the Spaten Brewery in Munich. Both made lager beer. Lager means storage place and the beers were stored or matured in cellars packed with ice that was cut from lakes and rivers until the invention of refrigeration. Lager beers were dark, the result of malt cured over wood fires. Dreher and Sedlmayr were aware of developments in England and were anxious to study the production of pale ale. They were generously treated in Burton.

Bass presented the visitors from Europe with saccharometers that enabled them to measure the fermentable sugars in wort. The visitors responded with acts of industrial espionage. They used thermometers to secretly measure temperatures and they had hollowed-out walking sticks with hidden valves in which they kept samples of beer and wort for later analysis. They wrote home saying that while they had been warmly welcomed in one brewery 'we still stole as much as we could'. 'It always surprises me that we can get away with these thefts without being beaten up,' Sedlmayr added. The young brewers were impressed in particular by the new methods of kilning grain to produce pale malt. When they returned home, Sedlmayr was at first slow to act, as deeply conservative Bavarian drinkers remained committed to dark or 'dunkel' versions of lager. Dreher kilned his malt to a paler colour and the result was a lager beer called Vienna Red, still darker than Burton beers.

The breakthrough came in Bohemia in 1842, where the Burghers' Brewery in Pilsen produced the world's first golden lager with the aid of a malt kiln imported from England. The beer was called Pilsner – 'of Pilsen' – and it proved a sensation. It was exported throughout the Austro-Hungarian Empire, with a special beer train leaving daily for Vienna. Pilsner was sold to the rest of Europe, Scandinavia and eventually to the United States with the 'second wave' of immigrants from Europe. As other brewers hurried to copy the Bohemian beer, it was given the full title of Pilsner Urquell, which translates as 'Original Source of Pilsen'. The advantages of golden lager over pale ale were obvious. The pale ales exported from Burton either in bottle or cask contained yeast sediment. They went through a secondary and even tertiary fermentation during the long sea voyages and, when they arrived at their destinations, the beers needed time to settle. Lager beer, on the other hand, has its second fermentation in the lager cellar in the brewery. The beer that emerges is bright, sparkling and ready to drink.

India Pale Ale came under attack. As early as 1858, an agent in Calcutta complained to William Younger in Edinburgh: 'Your beer is well known for its body. This is an obstacle to its becoming a favourite brand; it takes so long to ripen. The few casks of your last lot were fully 18 months before sufficiently ripe to drink'. That must have been an exception, for all the evidence suggests that most pale ales were ready to drink within weeks rather than months of when they arrived in India. But criticism was mounting. There were complaints from India about the soporific and narcotic nature of heavily-hopped pale ale. As the hop is a member of the same plant family as cannabis, the complaints may have had some justification. One colonial critic of the Burton beers said they had 'too much alcohol, too much sediment, too much hops and too little gas'.

This was not a view shared by all the British in India. Lord Curzon, the ruler of India between 1898 and 1905, recalled in his *Memoirs from a Viceroy's Notebook* the time when he was trekking through Afghanistan on horseback and was hallucinating about beer. 'As I rode down the grassy slopes, I saw coming towards me in the distance the figure of a solitary horseman… at that moment I would have given a kingdom, not for champagne or hock and soda, or hot coffee but for a glass of beer!' His wish was answered when the horseman arrived, pulled open his coat and handed Curzon a bottle of Bass Ale.

Nevertheless, lager beer made rapid inroads into what had been an almost monopoly overseas market for British brewers. In 1885, two Germans founded the Gambrinus Brewery in Melbourne. They were followed by the Foster brothers from the United States, who launched a second brewery in Melbourne dedicated to cold-fermented beer: they brought a refrigeration unit with them. Castlemaine started to brew in Brisbane in 1889. The following year, a Swiss brewer named Conrad Breutsch was invited to New Zealand specifically to produce lager. German brewers built lager plants in Africa and China. The Japanese became active in Asia while American brewers, when they arrived in India, came with ice as well as beer. Intrigued by this novelty, Indians realised they had their own supplies of ice on hand from their mountainous regions. The English had introduced both beer and cricket to India but now found themselves, metaphorically, on the back foot on a sticky wicket.

The *Brewers' Journal* in August 1882 castigated the big brewers, Bass, Allsopp, Barclay Perkins and Guinness, for not seizing the opportunity to dominate the world export market. 'Bottled Bass,' the journal thundered, 'has been found in every country where Englishmen had yet set foot', but now Bass and its competitors were failing to match the zeal of the Germans. The Burton brewers could have adopted lager production but, apart from the considerable cost involved in installing new equipment, there was also the matter of national pride. They stood in the engine room of a great industrial empire and had no intention of bowing the knee to rival brewers from central Europe. Echoing Martin Luther at the Diet of Worms, they declared: 'Here we stand, we can brew no other'.

This time there was no panic in Burton. Mr Allsopp didn't need to dine with Mr Marjoribanks, as the brewers had already established more lucrative trade on their collective doorstep: the domestic market. The costs of transport were far cheaper and from the 1840s it was possible to move beer around at speed using the new railway system; the impact of the train will be dealt with in the next chapter. Changes in society created growing demand for a pale beer among the new middle class that helped mark them out from the working class with their cheaper milds and porters. Pale ale cost around 7*d* or 8*d* a quart, compared to 4*d* or 5*d* for mild and porter. Richard Wilson, in *The British Brewing Industry 1830-1980*, argues that 'quality and cost… made it [Burton pale ale] a status drink for the expanding lower middle-class of clerks and shopkeepers, the armies of rail travellers, and those "aristocrats of labour" [highly-skilled workers] whose standards of living rose appreciably after 1850.' When duty on glass was lifted in 1845 and drinkers switched from pewter tankards to glass containers, Wilson says, pale ale 'became the high-fashion beer of the railway age.' The attractive clarity and sparkle of pale ale was aided by the development of the 'Burton Union' system that removed yeast towards the end of fermentation. The beer market also expanded as a result of the 1830 Beer Act that allowed any householder to sell and even make beer for an annual licence of two guineas. Within eight years, close to 46,000 new beer houses were added to the stock of 51,000 licensed inns, alehouses and taverns that existed before the Act passed into law. The spread of 'Tom and Jerry houses' – a slang term for dilapidated buildings – was to prove a double-edged sword for the Burton brewers but for a period the beer houses did offer an opportunity for increased sales.

Burton pale ale, a beer designed for export, arrived in Britain as the result of a shipwreck. In 1827, a ship carrying 300 hogsheads of India Pale Ale foundered off the coast of Liverpool in the Irish Sea. Both Allsopp and Bass claimed the consignment was theirs – a further example of Burton folklore. A Bass guidebook published in 1902 said: 'A quantity saved was sold in Liverpool on behalf of the Underwriters. The quality was so much appreciated that the fame of the new "India Beer" spread in a remarkably rapid manner throughout Great Britain.' That is an exaggeration. Sales of 'India Beer' were in fact slow to develop, and didn't grow until 1839 as a result of railway mania. There is also a major question mark hanging over this story: IPAs only reached drinkable condition following the lengthy journey to the sub-Continent. Beer drunk young from a shipwreck would have been neither pleasant nor bright in appearance. Perhaps advice was sought from Burton and Liverpool publicans were urged to mature the beer for a few months, a notion that tends to stretch credulity.

Whatever the truth of the shipwrecked beer, Burton brewers knew they had to refashion IPA for the domestic market. Export pale ale was in the region of 7 per cent alcohol and heavily hopped to avoid infections on the long sea voyages. The brewers had listened to their critics in India and also knew IPA was too strong and bitter for home consumption. The export beers were hopped at the rate of 6 pounds per barrel, more than twice the rate for domestic beers. Hop bitterness would have softened during the sea voyage but the beers would still have been extremely bitter to the taste, with an iodine or quinine character, and would have needed some time to become palatable. In Britain, with growing concerns about drunkenness, the first stirrings of a temperance movement and a middle-class desire for respectable behaviour, pale ale was not only hopped at around half the rate of IPA but was lowered in strength by around a quarter. As the century progressed, rising excise duties and genuine consumer demand for less alcoholic beer further drove down gravities.

During the 1840s, the output of Burton's breweries increased from 70,000 barrels a year to 300,000. Allsopp and Bass were jointly responsible for 70 per cent of that production. Between 1850 and 1880, the Burton brewing industry trebled in size every ten years. Brewers in London and other major industrial areas were desperate to win a share of the pale ale market as porter, once the biggest style in the country, went in to decline: porter production at Truman's and Whitbread in London fell by around 30 per cent in the early decades of the nineteenth century. The London brewers attempted to brew pale ale but met with mixed success. Several of them decided that the only course of action was to open breweries in Burton in order to take advantage of the mineral-rich spring waters of the Trent Valley. Ind Coope of Romford in Essex arrived in 1856 and built a brewery adjacent to Allsopp's (a useful site, as the two companies were to merge in 1934). Others were slower to follow, but the increasing success and profitability of their Burton competitors forced Charrington, Mann Crossman & Paulin, and Truman to move to the town. Provincial brewers followed in their wake. Boddingtons of Manchester, Alexander Walker and Peter Walker from Warrington, and Everards of Leicester set up in Burton: some, like Ind Coope, built new plants, others took over existing companies. In 1834 there were nine breweries in the town. The number rose to fifteen by 1851 and by 1888 there were no fewer than thirty-one breweries in Burton producing 3 million barrels of beer a year, compared to 80,000 barrels in the 1840s. As Peter Mathias noted above, Burton was now wholly a 'beer town' and had achieved the seemingly impossible: by the late nineteenth century it produced twice as much beer as London.

With the exception of Ind Coope, which continued to run breweries in Burton and Romford, most of the incomers were not especially successful. Manns enjoyed a fine reputation in London for its mild ale but it failed to produce pale ale that matched the quality of the local Burton brewers. The company was in Burton between 1872 and 1896 and in that time it created a 30-acre site with brewery, cooperage, stores, stables, wells and a model village for its workers. The village included twelve cottages, four villas, a head brewer's house and St Aidan's Church. John Crossman, a director of the company, said of the brief Burton venture: 'It came like a shooting star and quickly disappeared, paying the cost and leaving behind it a street named Crossman and a little church (endowed).' When Manns retired back to London, the site became the Albion Brewery Co. for just one year and was then bought by Marston, Thompson & Son, a company still on the site as Marston's, with the name of Mann Crossman & Paulin carved in the façade.

Truman, Hanbury & Buxton, a close neighbour of Manns in east London, was considered to make fine pale ale in Burton but still found it hard to compete with Allsopp and Bass. It turned to blending its London and Burton beers with a marked lack of success and eventually retreated back to Brick Lane in Whitechapel.

Marston's coopers posing with their casks in the nineteenth century.

As all the incomers, save for Ind Coope, returned to their natal towns they must have wondered whether the journey to Burton had been worth the effort, for further advances in science and technology meant they could soon brew pale ale in their original breweries. Louis Pasteur's work *Études sur la Bière* in 1876 taught brewers how to keep their breweries scrupulously clean to avoid yeast infections and spoilt beer. In 1883, Emil Christian Hansen in the Carlsberg laboratory in Copenhagen isolated a single strain of pure brewer's yeast that eradicated infected strains, which resulted in sour beer. Although his work was carried out for lager brewers, who had encountered major problems when they attempted to brew in the summer months, Hansen's work was also seized on by ale brewers, though not all of them reduced their yeasts to a single culture. Bass, for example, used a two-strain yeast culture that it believed produced the best-tasting beer.

Even before Pasteur published his findings, Allsopp had taken on a brilliant young German scientist, Dr Henry Böttinger, as the company's scientific adviser. Bass appointed John Matthews as its 'chemist and principal brewer' and he was joined by Cornelius O'Sullivan in 1865. O'Sullivan's outstanding work on the theory and practice of brewing won him many awards and in 1885 he was appointed a

Fellow of the Royal Society. It was his pioneering research that helped brewers move from seasonal brewing to year-round production. Dr Horace Tabberer Brown at Worthington carried out far-reaching research into barley germination, yeast nutrition and microbiology. He, too, became a member of the Royal Society. His half-brother, Dr Adrian Brown, worked for Thomas Salt until 1900, when he left to establish the British School of Malting and Brewing at the University of Birmingham. The brewing scientists in Burton formed a circle with the tongue-in-cheek name of the Bacterium Club. They were aided by the generous support of their employers, who paid them handsomely and made sure they had suitable space for laboratories and the most up-to-date equipment: Cornelius O'Sullivan was paid £3,500 a year by Bass, an enormous salary for the time.

The problem of disposing of excess yeast, which multiplies many times over during fermentation, and ensuring that pale ale was sparkling and not cloudy in the glass, was solved by the Liverpool brewer, Peter Walker, father of the Walker brothers mentioned above. His 'Burton Union' system is described at the end of the chapter. The most important development, arguably, was an understanding of the chemical qualities of Burton well water. Combrune and Richardson and later Molyneux and Shaw boiled off samples of Burton water to reveal the salts in solution. A chemist called C.W. Vincent taught brewers in London and elsewhere how to add such minerals as gypsum and magnesium to their brewing liquor to replicate Burton's water. Once it was possible to 'Burtonise' water, brewers throughout Britain were able switch to pale ale production with comparative ease.

Allsopp, Bass and the other Burton companies had seen off the incomers to the town, but they now faced increased competition as brewers everywhere added pale ale and India Pale Ale to their repertoires. But as the century came to a close, the Burton brewers enjoyed the advantage of their size, their good name and the ability of the railway network to deliver their beers nationwide. Ships had built them a global business. Now the iron horse enabled them to dominate their home country.

The Magic of Burton Water

Marston's Brewery draws more than 1 million gallons of water a week from wells near the Shobnall Road plant in Horninglow — a figure that emphasises the importance of water to the brewing process.

Water is created by rain falling on the earth. When it hits the earth, it drains through the top soil, percolates through layers of minerals and porous rock, and snakes and winds its way through cracks in non-porous rock until it settles on a table of impervious rock, where it waits to be collected. It may force its way back to the surface in the form of a spring or overflow into a river. Its formation will

Marston's Brewery in 2011, on a site built by Mann, Crossman and Paulin.

depend on the minerals present in the rocks and soils of a particular area. Soft water is the result of rain falling on insoluble rock such as granite or slate. Where soluble rock is present, water will pick up such sulphates as calcium and magnesium, also known as gypsum and Epsom salts. Calcium sulphate is highly beneficial to the brewing of pale ale. It helps create the correct level of acidity in the mash, known as the PH, short for 'power of hydrogen'. It also encourages enzymes in barley malt to convert starch into maltose during the mashing stage of brewing. Paul Bayley, the retired head brewer at Marston's, says Burton brewing 'liquor' plays a crucial role in the flavour and keeping qualities of pale ale. According to Bayley: 'Calcium reduces sugar and helps produce more alcohol. It keeps the yeast active, reduces haze, decreases beer colour and improves hop utilisation. The result is a more bitter beer. Magnesium acts in a similar fashion and sulphates give a drier flavour and enhance bitterness.'

The Trent Valley is 2 miles wide and was formed by glaciers and rivers over millions of years. In the bottom of the valley there are large deposits of gravel left by the action of the river. In the 1860s a remarkable man named William Molyneux endlessly tramped around the Trent Valley, analysing the soil, rocks and water of the area. He recorded his findings in *Burton-on-Trent; its History, its Waters, and its Breweries* in 1869. He discovered gravel, marl, coal, sand, shale, clay, Keuper

Marston's carry out a full range of activities on the site ranging from brewing to bottling.
Some such as cleaning Burton Union Sets and Bottling require a large volume of water
and in general it takes 7½ barrels of water to brew 1 barrel of beer.

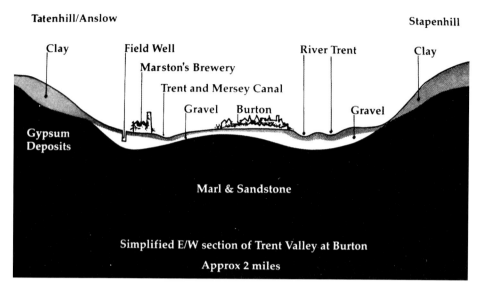

Diagram of the Trent Valley. and the well that supplies Marston's.

sandstone and Bunter sandstone. Where brewing is concerned, he reported:

> All the old wells of Burton are sunk in ordinary valley gravels, in a line running
> north and south, and principally on the east side of High Street. Until the year
> 1856 none of these wells exceeded twenty feet in depth; and except at one point
> in Anderstaff Lane, neither the thickness of the gravels, nor the nature of the
> strata upon which they rested, had been determined by actual experiment. In
> that year, however, by the assistance of powerful pumping machinery a well was
> carried to a depth of twenty-four feet on the premises of Messrs Ind, Coope and
> Co. in Station Street; and since that time it has become customary to deepen the
> old and carry all new wells connected with the breweries completely through
> the gravels to the underlying Keuper beds.
>
> In addition to the supplies of the ordinary wells, attempts have been made
> to obtain water by artesian borings into the different deposits upon which
> the gravels rest. In 1863 Messrs Bass and Co sunk a well through the gravels
> (twenty-six feet) into Keuper marls, in their New Brewery premises, Station
> Street, and by borings carried through the gypseous marls (seventy feet) obtained
> a fine supply of water from a bed of loose sand and gravel. Ninety yards north of
> this point in their Middle Brewery yard, the gravels were twenty-six feet thick;

and borings, carried down through 194 feet of gypseous marls with bands of hard sandstone, failed to produce more than a gallon of water during the hour.

Molyneux's findings show that the term 'Burton water' should be used with caution as there is a wide variation in the composition of the soil in the area and the quality of water extracted. At Marston's, for example, there are two series of wells on the site. The Field Wells supply water fit for brewing and it comes from five interconnected wells along the boundary of the brewery's sports field. But water from the Crossman Street wells on the Trent & Mersey Canal side at the rear of the site is fit only for cleaning. The brewery draws further cleaning water from a bore tube that draws water from 1,000ft.

In spite of these variations, Burton water is ideally suited for pale ale production. The most telling fact is the comparative level of salts present in water in two of the world's great brewing centres: Burton and Pilsen in the Czech Republic. The total salts in Burton water amount to 1,226 parts per million; in Pilsen, home of the first golden lager, where brewers want soft water to emphasise the malty character of their beer, the figure is just 30.8 parts per million.

Burton's wells can be dangerous. In the nineteenth century, a serving girl named Lizzie, working in the scullery of the brewery secretary's house at Marston's, suddenly found that the tiled floor had given way and she was in imminent danger of plunging into a well 35ft deep that contained 16ft of water. According to the *Burton Evening Gazette*, Lizzie grasped the leg of a table and managed to drag herself to safety. The newspaper did not record whether the water in the well was suitable for brewing or only for cleaning.

Burton water could also cause confusion. In 1830, the brewers in the town had to clear themselves of a serious accusation of adulterating their beers. The charge was made by the Society for Diffusing Useful Knowledge in its Treatise No. 60 on the 'Art of Brewing', which claimed that the Burton brewers added salt, steel, honey, prunella, jalap, sulphate of lime and black rosin. An application was made to the Court of King's Bench in February 1830 to bring libel charges against the publishers of the treatise. The case was disposed of when the publishers withdrew their statements. Counsel for the brewers, Mr Brougham, told the court that 'the author of the Treatise was, at the time his wrote his article, not aware that the springs at Burton ran over a rock of gypsum, which gave them a natural impregnation.'

A more damaging charge was made in 1852 by a French chemist named Payer, who said in a lecture on hygiene in Paris that the 'peculiar bitterness' of Burton pale ale was derived from the use of strychnine. The struggle to clear their name took the Burton brewers six months and they were supported by a vigorous campaign waged by the British press. The brewers opened their stores in Britain and throughout the world for inspection. In the end, no court action was required, as independent chemists and scientists concluded that the charge was without foundation. As William Molyneux drily observed, the claim by Monsieur Payer 'formed one of the best kind of advertisements the ale could possibly have had in creating a universal curiosity respecting it, and the desire to cultivate a closer acquaintance with a beverage admitted to be of so wholesome and genial a character'. Following the success the Burton brewers enjoyed at the Great Exhibition in London in 1851, the notoriety only added to the demand for their pale ale.

Strength of the Unions

The Burton Union system has nothing to do with trade unions, though (with unintended humour) the Transport & General Workers' Union once had an office next to the Union Rooms at Marston's. The system was devised to solve the problem of excess yeast created during fermentation and the need, once drinkers switched to glass containers, to ensure a clear and sparkling pint of pale ale.

The system was designed in 1838 by a Liverpool brewer, Peter Walker. He turned an old method known as the carriage cask on its head. The carriage cask was a messy and unhygienic system in which fermenting beer rose from the bungholes of casks, ran down the sides and was collected in troughs below. The beer was returned by jugs to the casks while most of the yeast was retained in the troughs.

Peter Walker's act of genius was simply to move the troughs above the casks and link them by pipes. In the carriage system, the casks were sent out to pubs but Walker developed large oak casks that remained in the brewery in what became known as Union Rooms. Each union cask holds 150 gallons of beer. The term 'union' comes from the fact that casks, trays and pipes are linked together, or 'held in union', as the Victorians said.

The pipes are connected to the bung holes of the casks and then rise up to the troughs, known as barm trays – barm is a dialect word for yeast in the Midlands and northern England. The pipes each have a 'swan neck' at the top so that fermenting beer and yeast, driven out of the bung holes by the force of fermentation, drip into the balm trays. The trays are held at a slight incline: the beer runs down the incline and returns to the casks via further pipes, while most of the yeast is retained in the trays. The yeast can then be used to make further batches of beer, or it can be sold to other brewers or to the Marmite factory handily sited in Burton.

Not all the yeast is cleared from the beer: sufficient is left to ensure a powerful secondary fermentation in the cask when it leaves the brewery. At Marston's, between 0.5 million to 1 million yeast cells per millilitre of yeast are left in the beer. In the pub cellar, yeast will drop to the base of a cask with the addition of isinglass finings that attract both yeast and protein.

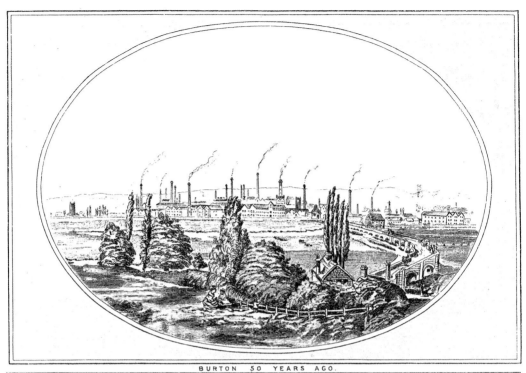

BURTON 50 YEARS AGO.

BURTON IN THE 18TH CENTURY.

Bucolic images of Burton in the eighteenth century, before the rapid growth of the town a century later.

In the nineteenth century, breweries throughout the country rushed to adopt Walker's union system. It was seized on with particular enthusiasm in Burton as the method helped produce the finest pale ales. It rapidly fell out of favour elsewhere as a result of the costs of maintaining and replacing the giant oak cask and the labour involved. Mechanical skimming devices were designed to remove yeast from fermenting vessels, but the Burton brewers remained faithful to unions well into the twentieth century. Today only Marston's uses unions and it promotes the advantages of a system used to produce its Pedigree pale ale. The former union sets from the Bass brewery stand forlornly in a car park alongside a visitor centre.

Surviving the Journey

India Pale Ale had to endure long sea journeys. In the nineteenth century, before filtration or pasteurisation, the beer would have contained yeast sediment that encouraged a second or even third fermentation in bottle or cask during the journey. One of the complaints from India about pale ale, as we saw above, was that it contained too much sediment. But yeast not only created further fermentations but also kept the beer free from infection. Paul Bayley, former Marston's head brewer, argues that yeast as much as alcohol and hops kept beer destined for India in good condition.

Nevertheless, fermentation created obvious problems: bottles or casks could break under pressure, causing havoc and mess in the holds of ships. This was avoided by trial and error. Peter Mathias says:

> Only the strongest malt liquor brewed would stand any chance of survival in the long journey through the tropics. Beer in the bottle probably did better than beer in casks, aided by being air-tight and under pressure through corking. Benjamin Wilson and Samuel Allsopp often advised customers to bottle the ale which they wanted to survive into the summer, leaving the bottle uncorked for a time to allow the ale to go flat. This was exactly the procedure adopted by a London wine merchant, Kenton, who is said to have first shipped porter successfully to the East Indies. Once 'flat', it was corked and sealed so that secondary and tertiary fermentation on the voyage brought it up to the necessary state of 'briskness' by the time it reached India.

Many brewers preferred to use casks. Casks for export were made with staves twice the thickness of those used for domestic trade. This can be seen in the Guinness Storehouse, its Dublin museum, where an old black and white film shows coopers preparing casks for Foreign Export Stout. When Burton casks reached their ports

Burton unions, still in use at Marston's brewery.

of embarkation in Liverpool or London, the bungs were loosened to allow the build up of carbon dioxide to vent and were then tightened again before the cask were loaded in the ships' holds. This method was verified by the late Dr John Harrison, brewing historian and founder of the Durden Park Beer Circle. Visitors to the National Brewery Centre in Burton can see the special porous venting plugs or 'shives' made of red oak that allowed further gas to escape on the voyage, while casks were criss-crossed at each end with staves of wood to stop explosions.

The tumultuous nature of the voyage was tracked in a brilliant piece of research by the American brewer and scientist Thom Tomlinson in 1994. Tomlinson at the time brewed an IPA called Renegade Red in Boulder, Colorado, and he worked with the Climate Diagnostics Center in Boulder to trace the temperatures that a shipload of ale would encounter on a voyage from Liverpool or London to India in the mid- to late 1800s. The research appeared in the March/April 1994 issue of *Brewing Techniques*, published in Eugene, Oregon. The ships left between late November and early February, arriving in India between March and May. The winter departures were timed to ensure the ships reached the Indian Ocean before the onset of the monsoon season. Heading south from England, the ships crossed the equator, cruised south along the coast of Africa, rounded the Cape of Good Hope and then crossed the Indian Ocean to Bombay, Calcutta, Madras and other ports of call. 'Even though the hogsheads [54-gallon casks] of ale were stored in the lowest level of the ship's hull – the coolest place in the ship – the temperature fluctuations were tremendous,' Tomlinson wrote. The research showed that for the first few weeks of the voyage, water temperatures were approximately 52 degrees Fahrenheit/11 degrees Celsius. As the ships entered equatorial regions, temperatures climbed to 81 degrees F/25 degrees C. As they rounded the Cape, temperatures dropped to between 65-69 degrees F/17-19 degrees C. In the southern part of the Indian Ocean water temperatures soared to 73 degrees F/21 degrees C. On the final leg of the voyage, nearing the coast of India, temperatures would reach 83-86 degrees F/26-28 degrees C. Tomlinson drily observed, 'Combine the temperature fluctuations and the rough waters off southern Africa and you have one hellish trip for ale.' He added that the 'hardy yeasts produced in Burton unions combined with high rates of priming sugar protected the beer on its stormy voyages and helped give it a long shelf life.' Priming sugar is added to casks as they leave the brewery and help encourage a strong second fermentation.

Brewers who sent pale ale in casks also supplied bottles and corks, so the beer could be bottled on arrival in India. As we have seen above, there were complaints from India about the length of time it took beer to settle and become bright. It's not known whether brewers sent finings with their beer; finings are made from isinglass and attract yeast and proteins in beer, dragging them to the bottom of casks. Beer in giant hogsheads and butts would have taken some time to 'drop bright' without the aid of finings. However, bottled beer would normally clear within a few hours.

One thing is certain: warm beer would not have been welcome in India. The problem was solved by placing bottles in a solution of water and saltpetre (potassium nitrate). Martyn Cornell, in *Beer: The Story of the Pint*, records that in 1828 a correspondent in India wrote to Samuel Allsopp telling him that in the hot season his beer was 'always cooled with saltpetre before it is drank: we can make it by this article as cold as ice'.

IPA: Back From the Dead

It's possible to trace and recreate nineteenth-century IPAs with greater confidence than Burton Ales as a result of surviving documents. Archivists at Bass claim that export ales brewed until the 1970s were based on recipes dating back to the 1850s. This means that Bass pale ale destined for India would have had an original gravity of around 1,060 degrees – or approximately 6 per cent alcohol. This is not exceptionally strong for the time but, assuming casks were primed with sugar and a vigorous second fermentation took place, the final level of alcohol would have been higher. The ales were heavily hopped in the brewing copper, between 4 and 6 pounds per barrel. Dry hops were added in the cask at around 6oz per barrel. The units of bitterness, had they been capable of measurement in the 1850s, would have reached seventy or eighty, almost twice as high as a modern pale ale or bitter, but hop bitterness would have softened during the voyage.

In 1993, Mark Dorber, who ran the White Horse pub in Parson's Green, south-west London, and who had a great passion for Burton pale ale, approached Bass and suggested the company should recreate an IPA. Bass was enthusiastic and called up a retired head brewer, Tom Dawson, for his advice. He recalled brewing a beer called Bass Continental for the Belgian market from the 1950s to the 1970s. The beer was based on recipes for Bass ale brewed in the 1850s and therefore represented an unbroken line with the original IPAs, which were all fermented with original gravities in the region of 1,063 degrees. Dawson consulted old brewing ledgers going back to the 1880s and drew up a recipe for the White Horse project. On 19 June 1993, a team of young brewers under Tom Dawson's guidance assembled at the Bass brewery in Burton to brew to Dawson's recipe, using a five-barrel pilot brewery designed to test new brews. The recipe was made up of 90 per cent Halcyon pale malt and 10 per cent brewing sugar. East Kent Goldings and Progress whole hops were used and were added at two stages during the copper boil. The hopped wort circulated over a bed of Progress in the collecting vessel following the boil for additional hop aroma. When the fermented beer was racked into casks, it was dry hopped with East Kent Goldings for aroma at the rate of 6oz per barrel. The yeast used was a two-strain Bass, one that dated from the time the company used union casks.

The beer reached 7.2 per cent alcohol with a literally stunning 83 units of bitterness – a modern bitter beer would have, at most, forty units. The bitterness was far more than Tom Dawson had planned but modern varieties of hops such as Progress are some 40 per cent higher in alpha acids than nineteenth century varieties. The beer was aged in casks for five weeks before it was served at the White Horse. I described it in the newspaper *What's Brewing* as having a:

> ...burnished gold colour. The colour rating is eighteen units. Placed next to a glass of modern Draught Bass and classic Pilsner Urquell lager beer, the White Horse IPA was mid-way between the two. The aroma was pungent and resiny. Hops dominated the palate and the long, intense bitter finish... Ripe bananas, pear drop and apple esters began to make themselves felt as the beer warmed up... Mark Dorber said the beer would remain in drinkable condition for some three months. Tom Dawson, with his long experience of Bass yeast, thinks it will survive for even longer.

Enthused by this experiment, Dorber and the author, with the support of the British Guild of Beer Writers, organised a seminar on IPA in London in 1994. We met in the historic surroundings of the Whitbread Porter Tun Room in Chiswell Street, with brewers from both Britain and the United States. Dr John Harrison outlined the history of the style and, to prove that IPAs could survive the journey to India, he said he had brewed a pale ale to a nineteenth-century recipe and kept it in his garage at a temperature of 80 degrees F/25 degrees C during a rare hot British summer in 1976. The beer was in good drinking condition the following Christmas. For the seminar, Dr Harrison presented a beer that was as close as possible to what he thought Hodgson's India Ale would have been like. He used Thames Valley well water and pale malt only, with no brewing sugars. The hops were East Kent Goldings with 5.5 per cent alpha acid, used at the rate of 2½oz per gallon and dry hopped at the rate of 0.5oz per gallon. It was fermented from an original gravity of 1,072 degrees, using a yeast strain from Truman's. The beer was six weeks old at the seminar and had been fined three weeks earlier. It had a powerful resiny aroma of Goldings hops; it was packed with tart fruit in the mouth and the finish was exceptionally dry and bitter, with a touch of astringency.

Those present at the seminar tasted two IPAs from Burton, brewed by Ind Coope and Marston's, one from the Castle Eden brewery near Hartlepool in North-east England, and three from the U.S.: Thom Tomlinson's Renegade Red (1,064 gravity, with a mouth-puckering 90 units of bitterness); Bombay Bomber (5.3 per cent alcohol), brewed by Teri Fahrendorf in Eugene, Oregon, where she added gypsum to her brewing water; and a 1,066 gravity beer brewed by Garrett Oliver at the Manhattan Brewery in New York City. There was great interest in the White Horse IPA, which by that time was eleven months old. Mark Dorber said that to counter the pronounced banana ester he had dry hopped the beer for a second time. The beer had become much softer. The fruitiness was almost

Madeira-like, with a pungent apricot fruit note on the nose, fruit, hops and nuts in the mouth and a big bittersweet finish.

To get a further glimpse of IPAs from the nineteenth century, I turned to James McCrorie, founder of the Craft Brewing Association, a home-brewers' organisation that recreates traditional beer styles and works closely with the Durden Park Beer Circle. James is a passionate devotee of IPA and the version of his I sampled in April 2011 was brewed in September 2009, making it twenty months old. It had an original gravity of 1,073 degrees and a finished strength of 7.8 per cent alcohol. James used a 50:50 blend of pale malt and lager malt. Only one hop, the East Kent Golding, was used at the rate of 2½oz per gallon. The beer had a bronze/ pale copper colour and a rich aroma of fresh tobacco, cracker-like malt, peppery hops and blood orange fruit. The fruit was rich and intense in the mouth, balanced by chewy malt and bitter hop resins. Malty sweetness was strong in the finish but tart fruit and intensely bitter hops prevented any cloying character. It was a wonderfully refreshing beer; James, in the finest traditions of the Raj, served the beer with kedgeree.

The IPA genie is out of the bottle. The guild seminar provoked such interest in the style that since 1994 hundreds of interpretations of IPA have appeared on both sides of the Atlantic.

Chapter Five

BEEROPOLIS

The railway transformed brewing in Burton. The first train steamed in to the town in 1839, linking Burton to the Birmingham and Derby line. The brewers now had easy access to England's Second City with its host of industrial workers demanding refreshing beer. The railway was one of the wonders of the industrial age. Thousands of miles of track were laid at a dizzy speed as navvies slashed and burned their way through the countryside. Industrialists saw the enormous benefits of moving their goods quickly around the country: freight, not passengers, was the first consideration of the early railway companies. Allsopp, Bass and their competitors found they could convey beer at a pace that would have seemed unimaginable when canals and coaches offered the only means of transport. Soon, most parts of Britain could be reached within a day. When St Pancras Station was opened in London in 1868, the Midland Railway brought Burton beer to the capital via Derby in a few hours. Bass rented a large warehouse close by with a capacity of 120,000 barrels and a workforce of 150 men, where the hogsheads were broken down into smaller casks and bottles for onward transmission to London's pubs. A year later, Bass moved this operation to the cellars of the station itself. The large space, known as the Undercroft, was designed by consulting engineer W.H. Barlow, who used iron columns and girders to maximise space. He said that 'the length of a beer barrel became the unit of measure, upon which all the arrangements of this floor were based'. The Undercroft is now the departure lounge for Eurostar passengers.

The cost advantages offered by the railway were enormous. Before the arrival of the train, it cost £3 to transport 1 ton of ale – approximately five barrels – to London for a journey that lasted more than a week. The same amount of ale was sent to London by train at a cost of 15s. The impact of fast transport, lower costs and higher profits was ground-breaking. Gourvish and Wilson tracked the astonishing growth: total production of beer in Burton increased from some 70,000 barrels a year in 1840 to 300,000 ten years later. Bass, forging ahead as the leading brewer in the town, saw its sales increase from around 40,000 barrels a year in the period between 1837 and 1842 to 148,000 in 1853. By 1860, Bass produced 341,527 barrels, placing it on a level with the largest London brewers. By 1867, it was brewing close to a million barrels a year, making it the biggest brewer in the world.

It is the growth of Bass in the second half of the century that is the great success story of the period. But the other Burton brewers also saw spectacular increases in production. Allsopp built a second brewery in 1860 opposite the railway station. In *Curiosities of Ale and Beer*, published in 1889, John Bickerdyke described the size and scope of Allsopp's New Brewery: it measured 375ft in length and was 105ft wide, and the union rooms held a total of 1,424 union casks, each one with a capacity of 695 gallons. The total number of union casks in both the old and new breweries was 4,500 and the two plants could cleanse 230,688 gallons of beer at any one time. Allsopp had a combined workforce of 1,600, including workers in its own maltings. At the peak of Burton's power there were no fewer than thirty-two maltings in the town, all soaking, germinating and kilning vast amounts of pale malt for the town's burgeoning brewers.

Thomas Salt remained a major influence: by 1886 the company was run by Henry Wardle, the MP for South Derbyshire, who was a member of the Salt family. Thomas Salt, when he turned to brewing, sank a well a quarter of a mile from his brewery in order to obtain suitable 'liquor'. He had four maltings in the town, with the major one at Wallsitch. Worthington carved out a distinctive niche by concentrating on high-quality bottled beers. Its White Shield pale ale is still brewed in the former Bass brewery now owned by Molson Coors and has enjoyed considerable growth in recent years. It remains a potent link with the original IPAs of the nineteenth century.

Ind Coope built a brewery that was as large as its original site in Romford. Bickerdyke recorded that its Burton brewery contained thirty-two malt bins, 'each as large as a small dwelling house', which stored 10,000 quarters of malt. The hop stores held 5,000 'pockets' (sacks). The brewery had six boiling coppers, the largest of which held 32,400 gallons of wort. The fermenting room had space for twenty-four 'squares' (open vessels), each one holding 500 barrels of beer. The stores in seventeen buildings were linked by tramways that were 8 miles in length. According to the assiduous Bickerdyke, Ind Coope employed thirty-two coopers, while twenty-three huge vats stored what he called 'old ale', probably the brewery's version of Burton Ale.

The 'Middle Yard' at the Bass brewery in the 1850s.

Bass was determined not to be outdone by Allsopp. It built not one but two new breweries: the Middle Brewery was added in 1853 and a third was created in 1864. The original Old Brewery by 1877 had been greatly extended and occupied a 45-acre site with thirty-two steam engines. By June 1865, the value of all Bass's breweries and other buildings amounted to £353,229. The new breweries were built to cope with genuine and massive demand. While the Baltic trade had been lost, Bass continued to be a major exporter of beer, with Bass Ale sold in fifty-eight countries. India remained an important market until the close of the century, but by the 1840s Bass was selling as much beer to Australia as it was to the sub-continent. Sydney was the main city supplied by Bass, but the company also had agents in Hobart and Launceston in Tasmania as well as Adelaide, Melbourne and the Swan River region of Western Australia. New Zealand was not neglected, and over the years Bass built up agencies in Java, the Cape of Good Hope, China, Hong Kong, Ceylon and Singapore. Bass Ale reached Boston, New York and San Francisco, Barbados and Trinidad in the Caribbean, and as far south as Chile, Guiana and Peru. Bass success abroad clearly riled Allsopp. In 1844, Allsopp launched an attack on its rival, accusing it of undercutting its prices in India and producing misleading figures about Allsopp's sales. Bass replied in measured terms, producing its own figures that showed that in the year ending October 1843 Allsopp's exports had fallen while Bass's had increased significantly. Only one of Bass's agents had attempted to undercut Allsopp's prices, an act that Bass deprecated. The most revealing aspect of this unedifying spat was that in the year ending June 1844, more than 40 per cent of Bass's production went overseas.

Bass's success at home and abroad led to many attempts by competitors to pass off their beers as though they came from the Burton brewer. This included various examples of brewers using imitations of the Bass Red Triangle symbol on the bottle labels. In 1855 the brewery took action against Thomas Salt's London agent for using fake Bass labels on its beers. A government Act of 1862 made it an offence to forge a trademark and this encouraged Bass to prosecute firms as far apart as Rio de Janeiro, Lisbon, Malaga and the Netherlands. Many of the forgeries were crude in the extreme but Bass was affronted in particular by skilful labels printed in Hamburg and used on bottles of German beer exported to North Africa. Assuming the German beer was lager, this was the ultimate if back-handed compliment paid to one of the foremost producers of English pale ale. Bass took immediate steps to protect its image when new trademark legislation was introduced on 1 January 1876. The company sent one of its clerical workers to wait all night on the doorstep of the registrar's office in London, in order to be at the front of the queue as soon as the office opened for business. As a result, the Bass Red Triangle was duly registered as the first official trademark in the country, to be used for its pale ale. Its Red Diamond logo was registered as the second official trademark for the brewer's Burton Ales; it brewed half a dozen versions of Burton Ale, ranging from No. 1 (still brewed today) through Nos 2 to 6. A third logo, a brown diamond for stout, became registered trademark No. 3. The other Burton brewers hurried to protect their logos. Allsopp registered its Red Hand symbol, while William Worthington followed with its Dagger and Shield.

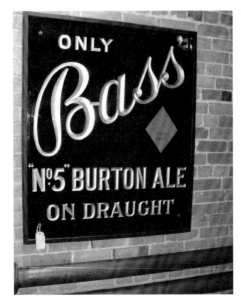

Plaque promoting Bass Burton Ale No. 5 – there were six different Burton ales to choose from.

The Bass Red Triangle, the first registered trademark.

Ind Coope's trademark was Britannia; Thomas Salt chose the Maltese Cross, and the Burton Brewery logo was the French Eagle. Later, Marston, Thompson & Evershed stayed closer to its roots with a trademark of the Staffordshire Knot.

Bass vigorously prosecuted firms at home and abroad who violated the brewery's trademarks. It sent its brewer and chemist Cornelius O'Sullivan on a tour of the country, appearing in court after court to prove that bottles bearing a Bass trademark were forgeries. The brewer's representative in Calcutta, Gillanders, Arbuthnot & Co., took court action against a number of rival companies passing off fake Bass products. Uncharacteristically, Bass did agree in 1876 to allow its Burton rival Ind Coope use of single and double diamond marks on its pale ales exported to India. Bass must have regretted this generosity when, a century later, Ind Coope developed one of the most successful ales in Britain named Double Diamond.

Domestic trade was booming due to the speed and cheapness of the railways. Michael Bass died in 1827 and he was succeeded by his son Michael Thomas, one of the most remarkable entrepreneurs and politicians of the century. In 1835, when John Ratcliff died, Michael Thomas Bass set up a new partnership with Samuel Ratcliff and John Gretton that created a company named Bass, Ratcliff & Gretton. Bass became the spearhead of the company and achieved national fame as the Member of Parliament for Derby for thirty-five years. He was a passionate supporter of the railway and helped create the first line through Burton in 1839. He followed this with investment in the Leicester to Burton line that increased the brewery's penetration of the Midlands region. He was a firm advocate of the 'liberal paternalism' of the Victorian age that believed that while working men should observe their dutiful place in a deeply class-ridden society, they should nevertheless be decently treated and remunerated. He took a great interest in the conditions of railway workers and before any journey by rail he would go to the front of the train and shake hands with the locomotive's driver and engineer. On one occasion, after a journey lasting some ten hours, he was angered to find the same men on the footplate. He discovered that railway workers were sometimes required to work eighteen and even twenty hours a day. Bass told the train company that unless they introduced shorter hours for their employees he would withdraw all his business from the line. The train company swiftly agreed to his terms. He gave financial help to the formation in 1871 of the first general trade union for railwaymen, the Amalgamated Society of Railway Servants, forerunner of the National Union of Railwaymen. The society invited Bass to be its first president, a position he politely declined. His motives in supporting the creation of the union were not entirely altruistic: first and foremost, he was concerned that his beer should be properly looked after on train journeys that took Burton pale ale as far as Cornwall in the south and Scotland to the north.

Bass & Co.'s Dixie Sidings, where casks of beer were loaded on to railway trucks.

Train that took Bass beer from the brewery to the main Midland line en route to all parts of Britain. On view at the National Brewery Centre.

The railway and Victorian paternalism joined forces to give Bass employees memorable annual day trips to the coast. Starting with a small outing to Liverpool in 1865, the trips developed into massive events that, according to Richard Stone in *Burton upon Trent: A History*, were organised with 'military precision', not too surprising as the first event was run by Captain John Anderson, a former police superintendent.

Only the largest resorts could cope with the sudden influx of around ten thousand visitors. Four main destinations were visited in rotation: Liverpool, Blackpool, Great Yarmouth and Scarborough. Up to 17 trains ran at ten-minute intervals from as early as 3.45am with the last train home not arriving until 2.30am the following morning.

When they reached their destination, the workers would be greeted by brass bands and would then board cruise ships for a short sea trip. In the afternoon, they sat down to a dinner, where they were joined by the chairman and vice-chairman of the brewery. The other leading Burton brewers followed Bass's lead in organising annual railway excursions for their employees, which continued until the outbreak of the First World War.

Trains also brought badly-needed seasonal workers to Burton. Brewing by the late nineteenth century was a year-round activity but some work, malting in particular, remained seasonal, with furious activity taking place after the annual harvest. In East Anglia, agricultural labourers were laid-off following the harvest and they needed other work in the autumn and winter. Bass, Allsopp and the other brewers gave the labourers return tickets to travel by train to Burton where they were given lodgings and also three-piece suits and jaunty caps for their leisure time. Depending on which county they came from, they were known colloquially as Norkies or Suffolk Jims. As well as wages, they were given copious amounts of free beer during their long sessions in the malting, where temperatures rose as high as 215 degrees Fahrenheit.

But the train was used primarily to move beer rather than men. To the annoyance of many Burton citizens, the brewers built their own network of lines that carried beer in wagons to the railway station and returned with raw materials and empty casks. In May 1858, it was estimated that 'floaters' – small tank engines – made their way to and from the station from dawn until dusk, carrying 1,000 tons or 186,800 gallons of beer a day. A year later, an Act of Parliament allowed the Midland Railway to build lines from Horninglow to the centre of the town, with a link to Allsopp's brewery. Further Acts allowed Bass to build track from the Midland Railway's line to its breweries, malthouses and cooperage. Later extensions linked premises to the east and west of Guild Street. In 1863, Bass's railways were valued at £6,684 and a further four locomotives were bought a year later. By 1865, Bass was one of the Midland's main customers, sending more than 100,000 tons of ale a year in 36,000 wagons, with a monthly freight charge of around £17,000. Bickerdyke, in 1889, described Burton as a town in thrall to the railway. Bass alone had 12 miles of track, with 60,000 trucks carrying 600,000 casks of beer a year, made up of butts and hogsheads. 'Piled one above another, they would make 3,300 pillars, each reaching to the top of St Paul's [cathedral].' He reported that Bass employed 2,250 men and boys: in 1821, only 827 men and 61 boys had been employed in all the town's breweries. In the same year, 1865, evidence of Bass's massive presence in the home market was measured by the fact that only 10 per cent of its production now went for export.

The crowded nature of Burton, with its ever-growing jumble of railway tracks and level crossings, prevented other industries setting up in the town. The problem was caused by the iron grip on much of the land in and around Burton exercised by the Marquess of Anglesey and other aristocratic landlords. Two centuries after the Cromwellian revolution, feudalism was still a powerful force in Burton. The landowners refused to grant freehold tenures and retained land on a leasehold-for-life basis that deterred entrepreneurs from bringing new business to the town. The policy was moderated in 1863 when fixed-term leases for ninety-nine years were introduced. Much of Anglesey's freehold in the built-up areas of Burton was relinquished in the early years of the following century, enabling new industries, including tyre manufacturers who met the demands of a nascent car industry, to set up in business. Anglesey's surviving estate of 5,091 acres was finally sold in 1918, but the landowners had lost political power some time before. When the Marquess opened a new bridge over the Trent in 1864, it was the last public ceremony performed by a member of his family. Burton became a municipal borough in 1878 and the first mayor was a brewer, William Henry Worthington. Six of his fellow aldermen, including Samuel Allsopp, Michael Arthur Bass, Sydney Evershed and Henry Wardle, were brewers, too. Their political influence spread beyond Burton. Several brewers followed Michael Thomas Bass and Henry Wardle into parliament. Samuel Allsopp was the member for Worcestershire while Michael Arthur Bass, son of Michael Thomas, was elected to represent Staffordshire East in 1868; he moved to the newly created seat of Burton in 1885. The new model economy had triumphed.

The extent of that triumph can be seen in a pamphlet entitled *A Glass of Pale Ale*, published in 1880, which was an extended version of an article in the *Daily News* in 1872. The piece is frustratingly anonymous, as newspapers did not give writers 'by-lines' or credits at that time. It gives a graphic portrait of Bass as a vast Victorian enterprise. It also serves as a fine description of the brewing process of the day. The writer reported that William Bass had started his company little more than a century before on an acre of land. In 1880, the Bass empire occupied 140 acres; it used 267,000 quarters of malt a year, 36,000 hundredweight of hops, and paid £300,000 to the government a year in excise duty. Weekly wages amounted

4 STEAM COOPERAGE, BASS'S BREWERY, BURTON-ON-TRENT

The camera as well as the train reached Burton in the nineteenth century.

to £2,500. 'Bass has in use 47,000 butts, 160,000 hogsheads, 140,000 barrels and 200,000 kilderkins; a stock of casks in all, in store and scattered over the country, exceeding half a million'.

The writer's description of the brewing process stresses how all the new technologies of the Industrial Revolution had been assimilated. When the wort was run off through the slotted base of the mash tun, 'the malt left is "sparged" by a shower bath of hot water to extract from it the last remains of saccharine-matter'. The wort is pumped by steam power to the coppers where hops are added and the wort is boiled. It then has to be cooled prior to fermentation. The writer noted that before the arrival of refrigeration, the temperature was often too high to allow fermentation to take place. But now the hopped wort is pumped to heat exchangers: 'It is difficult to make these out to be anything else than huge boxes; but by climbing up and peeping over the edge, we see a shallow lake, laced by successive long straight coils of copper piping... the boiled wort is flowing slowly from the coolers through this mighty submerged snake, while the cold water that covers it has given to it a slow, steady motion at right angles to the flow of the wort, so as to intensify the refrigerating power.'

Once fermentation has started, the fermenting wort is transferred from open vessels called squares to the great Union Room, where it continues to 'work' or ferment inside large wooden casks linked together by one long pipe. 'What a ballroom would this Union Room make if its floor were clear,' the writer noted, 'but instead of dancers it holds 2,500 casks, each one containing 160 gallons'.

Behind this glowing testimony to the power and modernity of Bass, storm clouds were beginning to gather over Burton. Changes that would impact on the brewers included the political influence of the temperance movement, the growth of the 'tied trade' and increased excise duties that cut brewers' profits. The town was dubbed 'Beeropolis... a very City of Beer' by one visiting writer at the turn of the century and it remained the undisputed brewing capital of the world, but its hegemony was beginning to come under attack at home and abroad. All brewers, not just in Burton, had been affected by the Beer Act of 1830, referred to in the previous chapter. As the number of new beer houses proliferated, the result was summed up by the Dean of St Paul's, the Revd Sydney Smith: 'Everybody is drunk. Those who are not singing are sprawling. The sovereign people are in a beastly state'. The Liberal and Whig supporters of the legislation were driven by a three-pronged passion: to introduce a completely free market for the sale of beer; to break the power of the licensing magistrates, who were believed to be in the pocket of the brewers; and to halt the growth of the tied trade in pubs. The tie meant that a pub was either directly owned by a brewer or tied to it through generous loans. The tie was a particular problem in London, where many pubs were controlled by the major brewers who then met in regular conclaves to fix prices. Tied pubs were less in evidence outside the capital. In Burton, for example, Allsopp, Bass and the other brewers owned few pubs but preferred to sell their beer through agencies set up throughout the country.

The Beer Act backfired in every way. Far from weakening the power of the brewers, it intensified the spread of the tied house. The new beer houses were not only poor places but most of the owners were incapable of producing decent ale. Many of them found it difficult to pay the annual licence, let alone invest in brewing equipment that would brew bright and hygienic beer. By 1836, beer house producers accounted for around 13.4 per cent of total beer production but the figure had fallen to less than 10 per cent by 1860. As customers rejected the rank beer on offer, the owners of beer houses turned increasingly to commercial brewers for their supplies. The brewers' response to a beer house owner or tenant was a simple one: we will supply beer and offer loans to improve your premises but in return you will agree to take your beer only from one supplier. A new Beer Act in 1869 ended the rush to a complete free-for-all in the supply of ale. Licensing of all premises was firmly back in the hands of magistrates, who shared the Revd Smith's distaste for the 'sovereign people' and were swayed by

Proud Bass coopers posing with their handiwork.

the growing cacophony of the temperance organisations. The most vocal was the United Kingdom Alliance, which favoured total prohibition. Restrictions on both the availability of licences and pub opening hours sent thousands of Tom and Jerry houses out of business: it was only bigger beer houses, able to make tolerable beer, that survived. The collapse of many beer houses created a crisis for brewers who had loan tied these outlets. In 1896 Barclay Perkins, the biggest London brewer, was owed £2 million by bankrupt publicans, a colossal sum for the time. In Burton the situation proved catastrophic for Allsopp. It was widely viewed in the financial world as a badly-run business and the debts it had run up as a result of loans to publicans forced it into receivership and restructuring. Some of the company's decisions were startling: it spent £60,000 on a lager brewery when the demand for lager beer in England was tiny and it also invested £200,000 in the Kursaal funfair in far-off Southend-on-Sea in Essex.

Allsopp was rescued by a public floatation, a new form of ownership that had stunned the brewing world in 1886 when Guinness in Dublin became a public company. Guinness, in common with Bass, was a brewing phenomenon. With a tiny home market, it expanded into Britain with such success that the words 'stout' and 'Guinness' became synonymous. Its Foreign Extra Stout challenged Bass Ale as the most popular beer exported from the British Isles. It owned no pubs but its strict control of agents and bottling companies meant its Double Stout was invariably sold in excellent condition in Britain. Its £6 million floatation on the stock market enabled it to expand still further and to enlarge and improve its Dublin plant. By the end of the nineteenth century it had overtaken Bass to become the biggest brewer in the world, an achievement all the more remarkable at a time when demand for porter in England had been falling like a stone. English brewers rushed to follow Guinness's example, with Bass, Ratcliff & Gretton going public in 1888 with a share capital of £3.2 million and Michael Thomas Bass as chairman.

Limited companies played a different role in England to Ireland: the English brewers needed investment from shareholders in order to buy pubs and establish tightly-controlled tied estates. The rush for property was now on and prices soared as brewers scrambled to buy pubs and tie them hand-over-fist to their products. The example of Worthington is revealing. It had avoided owning pubs and, in common with Allsopp and Bass, had built an agency system throughout the country. By 1875, it had two warehouses in London, including one at St Pancras, with a joint capacity of between 3,000 and 4,000 barrels. By 1890 it had moved its London base to Broad Street with a much-expanded storage facility, where thirty horses delivered 1,000 barrels a week – a quarter of its annual output – to London pubs. It was also building sales of its bottled Worthington E and White Shield brands as the take-home market started to grow. But, along with Bass, it found itself frozen out of the growing number of pubs in the capital that were either owned directly by the big London brewers or tied to them through loans. As a result, both Bass and Worthington reluctantly joined the race to buy property at inflated prices: hence the need for capital investment from public floatation. Competition became cut-throat and resulted in a wave of mergers that created bigger brewers with the money and the muscle to survive. In London, for example, the merger of Watney, Combe and Reid created the biggest brewery in the capital. In the West Country, four breweries merged to form Bristol United Breweries, while in the Scottish capital Edinburgh United Breweries was a similar merger of four producers.

Mergers would affect Burton later, but in 1880 the brewers in the town were hit by changes to excise duty that increased their costs. William Gladstone, who combined the roles of Prime Minister and Chancellor of the Exchequer, dramatically changed the way beer was taxed in his 1880 Licensing Act. He introduced what he called the 'free mash tun' by removing the duty on malt and replacing it with a tax on beer. Gladstone said he was helping the brewers by allowing them to use cheaper ingredients, such as rice or maize, alongside barley malt. Duty would be levied on the original gravity (OG) of beer, a measure of the 'fermentable materials' in the mash tun prior to fermentation. As with most changes to taxation, the advantages offered by Gladstone proved to be a snare and a delusion. The new duty was levied at 6s 3d per standard barrel at an OG of 1,057 degrees, with a higher charge for stronger beer and a lower one for weaker products. When the brewers' accountants did their calculations, they discovered they would have to pay almost 1s a barrel more compared to the old malt tax. Big London brewers such as Truman responded by lowering the gravities of their mild ale and using large amounts of sugar. The Burton brewers were determined to maintain the high standard of their pale ales and in general avoided the use of inferior grains. In order to cut costs and maintain profits, however, they searched the world for cheaper barley and hops and started to import substantial amounts from Europe and North America. In 1897-8, for example, Colin Owen records that 23 per cent of the barley malted in Burton was made up of Smyrna grain from Turkey, 16 per cent from North Africa and 10 per cent from California. This was bad news for British farmers, two-thirds of whose annual barley crop was normally turned into malt for brewers.

Michael Thomas Bass died in 1884. He remained a Liberal to the end, though he was increasingly at odds with his party over its support for temperance and even heavier taxes on brewing. He was an active MP and regularly lobbied government ministers in support of the brewing industry. He was praised by Gladstone when he died, praise Bass would have rejected as he did not consider Gladstone to be a friend of the industry. One newspaper obituary, reaching for the hyperbole, said Michael Thomas Bass would live on in people's memories long after Disraeli and Gladstone had been forgotten. Bass's son Michael Arthur took over the reins as chairman of the brewing company, though as an MP he later resigned from the Liberal Party in protest against its anti-brewer and pro-temperance positions. Michael Arthur, who was made a baronet and then ennobled as Baron Burton, maintained his father's powerful paternalistic instincts. Football, tennis and cricket grounds were built in the town for the workforce, a free library and Post Office savings bank were made available and sick workers were sent to convalescent homes. Employees injured at work were given three months' pay, while long-service workers were provided with houses or cottages at peppercorn rents. At Christmas, all grades of workers, from managers to boys, were given gifts of beef, turkeys, geese, ducks, fowls, pheasants and hares. In return, the workers were expected to be loyal and dutifully to vote for their bosses when they stood for parliament or the local council.

But times and attitudes were changing. Michael Thomas Bass always claimed he paid his workers generously but figures quoted by Colin Owen show that in 1880 the average weekly wage at Bass was just £1 for a fifty-four-hour week. Some general labourers were paid as little as 17s. The firm's total expenditure on wages and salaries accounted for just 8 per cent of total costs and it seems that Michael Thomas Bass's concern for the plight of railwaymen did not spread to his own workers. With the exception of the coopers, who were well-organised and comparatively well paid, most of the Bass workers were slow to join Trade Unions. But in 1890 workers from all the town's breweries attended a mass meeting to discuss joining the Workers' Union. They carried resolutions calling for shorter hours and better wages. The Burton & District United Trades Council was set up the following year. In 1892, protesting against the bullying attitude of a new

Shobnall Ale Bank, scene of workers' unrest in 1892.

general manager, Herbert Couchman, Bass workers in the Shobnall department downed tools and marched to both the Old and Middle Breweries, where they urged their fellow workers to join them on strike. A mass meeting in the market place was supported by more than 400 men – and two-thirds of them voted for strike action. The dispute was resolved when John Gretton from the board of directors met a delegation of strikers and as a result the high-handed Couchman was told to improve his handling of the workers.

In 1893, a general meeting of brewery labourers organised by Burton Trades Council attacked 'starvation wages and cantankerous employers'. The meeting was widely reported in the press and caused disquiet in the board rooms of the local breweries. In the same year a large meeting of maltsters in Derby agreed to demand better contracts from their bosses. Progress was slow, but by 1911 a Burton branch of the Workers' Union was formed and in 1914 agreement was reached with the brewers to pay a standard wage of 23s for a fifty-four-hour week, with additional payments for piece work and overtime – scarcely a king's ransom.

The close of the nineteenth century saw a fundamental shift in the type of beer being brewed in England. It marked a sharp move away from beers such as IPA and porter that had to be stored or vatted for several months. Brewers switched production to what were dubbed 'running beers'. In cask, these beers could be served within a few days of leaving the brewery or were immediately available for consumption in bottle. E.R. Moritz, consulting chemist to the Country Brewers'

Society, wrote in the *Brewers' Almanack* of 1895: 'It is essentially within the last ten years that these lighter ales, both of pale and mild character, have come especially to the front. The public is in this period has come to insist more and more strongly upon extreme freshness of palate with a degree of brilliancy and sparkle their fathers never dreamt of.' In 1905, Julian Baker wrote in *The Brewing Industry*, 'the light beers, of which increasing quantities are being brewed every year, are more or less the outcome of the demand of the middle classes for a palatable and easily consumable beverage. A good example of this type of beer is the so-called "family ale", and the cheap kinds of bottled bitter beers and porters.'

There's a degree of sophistry in both these arguments. It's true that the rapidly-increasing middle class, desperate to appear respectable and a cut above industrial workers, preferred a type of pale ale that could be drunk either in the smart lounge bar of a pub or in the home. But in general the move towards beer that could be drunk young and fresh rather than well-matured came from the brewers and their shareholders, not the general public. The new pale ales were the result of scientific research and practice. All brewers could now 'Burtonise' their brewing water. Treated with sulphates, brewing liquor contributed to better extraction of malt sugars, improved hop utilisation and cleaner fermentation. Malting had been greatly improved and the move to pale malt meant that more sugary extract could be produced from smaller amounts of grain. The greater scientific understanding of yeast was also a powerful impetus to producing running ales. Pure strains meant fermentation could be better controlled. Yeast packed down and cleared in casks within a few days, enabling beer to 'drop bright' and be served within a day or two of reaching the pub cellar.

The major pressure on brewers to produce running beers came from shareholders. Big brewers, including Bass and Allsopp, were now limited companies and their shareholders expected a return on their investment. The days when a hogshead of IPA could quietly mature for six months were long gone. As Allsopp knew only too painfully, shareholders could raise merry hell at annual meetings if a substantial dividend were not paid. Competition became intense both within and without Burton. The Burton brewers were at first reluctant to buy pubs and preferred to offer publicans generous loans if they sold Burton pale ale. In 1891, Worthington reported that Allsopp was offering discounts of 22 per cent in South Wales, Salt 25 per cent in Manchester and Scotland, and Evershed 27 per cent. Bass and Worthington, who were to merge in the 1920s, were bellicose rivals in the 1890s, even resulting to legal action to defend their territories – Gourvish and Wilson say 'a seething hostility persisted'. The level of discounts – often as large as £5,000 to one pub – and the impact on profits, forced the Burton brewers to re-think their policy. In 1883, Bass owned just twenty-seven pubs throughout Britain and just fourteen in London. Allsopp owned no pubs in 1887 and its chairman told the company's first annual shareholders' meeting that it did not intend to go down the tied house route. But Allsopp did a complete volte face in the 1890s, raising £950,000 to buy pubs. The *Economist* magazine said the prices Allsopp's paid for pubs were 'insane' but, undaunted, the brewery increased its share issue by the astonishing sum of £3,250,00 to fund its frantic bid to build a large pub estate. The century ended with Allsopp owning 363 pubs and Bass 500. Worthington was no slouch in buying pubs, too. In 1896, Bass's London agent reported that Worthington was paying 'big prices' for pubs in the capital: £40,000 for the Priory in Clapton, £63,000 for the Woolpack in Moorgate, and £65,000 for a pub under the very office of Bass's agent.

As a result of these acquisitions, the Burton brewers were as conscious as their investors of the need to produce beer ready for sale within days. They were aided by the development of a new type of malt called crystal. This is 'stewed malt', made in a similar fashion to toffee. It arrives in the brewery with its starches already turned to sugar. It cannot be fermented but a small amount gives finished beer 'mouth feel' and body that masks its lack of maturation. Served on draught in pubs, this new type of beer was dubbed 'bitter' by drinkers and a style was born, the forerunner of today's cask-conditioned 'real ales'. The term bitter was scarcely ever used for bottled beer, which continued to be known as pale ale or by the new term of light ale.

Within a decade, many brewers, including Whitbread in London, were filtering, pasteurising and carbonating bottled beers. Bass and Worthington preferred to remain true to their roots and their Bass Red Label and White Shield beers continued to be 'bottle conditioned' with live yeast. But the century closed with a profoundly different brewing industry. The Burton brewers were under pressure from equally large competitors, formed by mergers and takeovers, which were now capable of producing pale beers that had appeared to be beyond their reach just a few decades earlier. India Pale Ale seemed a detail of history as the Burton brewers entered a new century with unaccustomed uncertainty.

The Burton Beerage

The ironic name 'the Beerage' was coined in London in the eighteenth century when Samuel Whitbread and other big porter brewers became rich and politically influential. A century later, the major Burton brewers were of equal status to their peers in London and the likes of Bass and Worthington had come a long way in a short time from their family roots as humble carriers and coopers. By the 1880s, at least two of the partners in Bass, Ratcliff & Gretton – Michael Thomas Bass and Richard Ratcliff – were millionaires.

Michael Thomas, when he succeeded his father at the brewery, lived at first in the family home on Burton High Street but he moved in the 1840s to Holly Bank (later renamed Hollyhurst) in Barton-under-Needwood. He moved again to Byrkley Lodge in Tattenhill and later built a substantial house at Rangemore, also in Tattenhill, where he died in 1884. His son, Michael Arthur Bass, was created a baronet in 1882 and was elevated to the peerage in 1886 as Baron Burton. Before joining the brewery, he had been educated at Harrow and Cambridge. As well as Rangemore, Lord Burton had a mansion in London's Mayfair, Chesterfield House, and he paid the Earl of Dudley £7,000 a year to lease the large Glenquoich estate in Scotland, which extended from Fort Augustus to the coast and provided facilities for shooting, fishing and the use of Loich Quioch Lodge. The Prince of Wales, later Edward VII, stayed at Rangemore, Mayfair and Glenquoich on several occasions. Henry Allsopp moved to Foremark in Derbyshire in the late 1840s and in 1860 transferred to Hindlip in Worcestershire, where he was appointed Lord of the Manor. He became Lord Hindlip in 1886, the year before he died.

Albury House in Stapenhill was built in the 1860s by Sydney Evershed while William Worthington died in 1871 at Newton Park in Newton Solney, later the home of Robert Ratcliff, who died in 1912.

The brothers John and Frederick Gretton were left a fortune by their father. John worked assiduously in the brewery but also developed a love of racehorses, large houses and yachts. The eldest of his three sons became the first Lord Gretton. Frederick Gretton's contribution to the firm was brief and ended in scandal: in 1872, at the age of thirty-three, he ran away to Paris with a sixteen-year-old actress

Aerial view of Rangemore Hall, seat of Lord Burton.

Workers at Bass Burton in the early years of the twentieth century.

named Fanny Lucy Radmill. When Frederick died at the early age of forty-two, in 1882, he owned houses and stables in many parts of the country, including a home in Belgrave Square in London. He also owned a steam yacht that was stocked with 2,000 bottles of wine and spirits (but apparently no bottled Bass) and a further 7,000 bottles were discovered at Bladon House near Burton. He berthed two smaller boats at Cowes, Isle of Wight, held the lease of a shooting lodge in Scotland and had 3,999 £1 shares in the family brewery. When his enormous debts were settled, his estate was still worth £235,000.

Hamar Bass, second son of Michael Thomas, was – to use a Victorian euphemism – 'a disappointment to his father'. He was educated at Harrow and was granted just one share in the brewery when he joined it. His lack of interest in brewing was all too evident but he nevertheless negotiated substantial loans from the company to pursue his other interests, which were mainly riding to hounds and buying a string of racehorses. He was elected to parliament as the Liberal member for

Tamworth, where he was notable for his eccentric behaviour (such as leaving late night sessions at Westminster to catch the milk train home in time for an early hunt the following morning). He won the Ascot Gold Cup in 1897, but died the following year as a result of a heavy fall while hunting. In spite of his tenuous links to the family brewery, he died a rich man, with an estate valued at £196,547 and shares in the brewery worth £600,000.

The wealth of the brewers enabled them to become generous benefactors in Burton. They endowed churches, built swimming baths and created a large number of athletic, cricket and football fields throughout the town. In 1894, Michael Arthur Bass gave the Liberal Club and St Paul's Institute, built by his father, to Burton to serve as the town hall. The Beerage had put its indelible stamp on Beeropolis.

Michael Thomas Bass.

Chapter Six

Wars and Recession

When the new monarch, Edward VII, stayed with Lord Burton at his country estate at Rangemore in 1902, the king seemed to set the seal on the power and privilege of the Burton beerage. The next day, the king toured the Bass breweries where he started a mash of No. 1 Ale, which was renamed King's Ale and sold commercially for £5 a barrel. But the start of the Edwardian era signalled the end rather than the consolidation of the Bass family grip on its brewing empire. Lord Burton died in 1909, and he didn't leave an heir. His nephew, William Arthur Hamar Bass, was as unsuited to running a business as his father, Hamar Bass, had been. He ran into severe financial problems as a result of his fixation with racehorses – a common trait among the Burton brewers – as well as other ill-thought-out enterprises. When he sold his shares in Bass, the company was firmly in the hands of the Grettons and the Ratcliffs. They were competent managers but they lacked the flair and drive of the Bass dynasty, Michael Thomas in particular.

Along with the other Burton brewers, Gretton and Ratcliff faced an increasingly hostile environment. The Liberal Party, dominated by David Lloyd George, whipped up the temperance movement into a frenzied campaign against the evils of drink and the public house. At the same time, competition among brewers intensified as the number of public house licences fell from 104,792 to 88,445 between 1886 and 1914, at the same time as the population grew by 45 per cent. During the same period, the proportion of pubs that were tied to suppliers rose from 75 per cent to 95 per cent, leading to trench warfare among the brewers to control the remaining 5 per cent. The need for additional investment and falling sales led to mergers and takeovers that saw the number of commercial brewers in Britain fall from 17,110 in 1881 to just 6,719 by the end of the century.

Lord Burton, a leading member of the Burton 'beerage'.

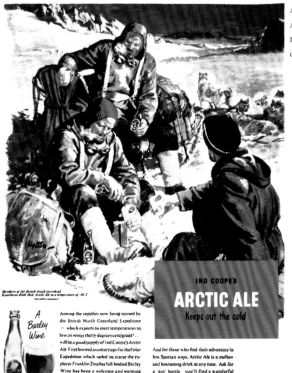

A short-lived promotion for Arctic Ale, which Allsopps resurrected in the twentieth century.

IND COOPE'S
ARCTIC ALE
Keeps out the cold

A Barley Wine

Among the supplies now being carried by the British North Greenland Expedition – which expects to meet temperatures as low as minus thirty degrees centigrade! ... will be a good supply of Ind Coope's Arctic Ale. First brewed a century ago for the Polar Expedition which sailed to rescue the explorer Franklin, This fine full-bodied Barley Wine has been a welcome and warming influence on many such expeditions since

And for those who find their adventure in less Spartan ways, Arctic Ale is a mellow and heartening drink at any time. Ask for a 'nip' bottle you'll find a wonderful strength in a small volume!

IND COOPE'S ARCTIC ALE *BY THE BREWERS OF* DOUBLE DIAMOND

Bruce Wilkinson and Geoff Mumford at Burton Bridge Brewery.

Marston's head brewer
Emma Gilleland.

Right: Guides in
Victorian dress at the
National Brewery
Centre.

Below: John Mills at
Tower Brewery.

James McCrorie with his home-brewing equipment; James recreated a Victorian IPA.

Martin Hodson (left) and Jack Morgan at the Black Hole Brewery.

John Saville at Old Cottage brewery.

Worthington's Jolly Angler.

Marston's beer mat.

Marston's coopers, who repair the union casks.

Cutaway of Marston's brewery, showing the brewing process and the union casks.

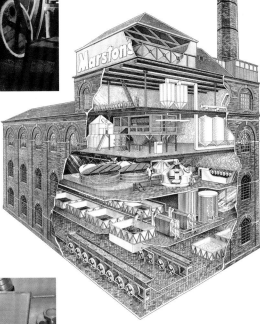

Matthew Otley brewing the special Burton Ale at Otley Brewery in South Wales.

Nick Otley of Otley Brewery.

919   Burton-on-Trent. Breweries from the River.

The Trent Valley: the vital link to Burton brewing.

Ind Coope was one of several southern breweries that built plants in Burton to make pale ale.

Worthington's Brewery, Burton-on-Trent

Worthington's Brewery, in Burton on Trent.

Bass & Co.'s Dixie Sidings, Burton-on-Trent

Bass & Co.'s Dixie Sidings.

Steve Wellington and Jo Wright in the Worthington Brewery.

Steve Wellington at the National Brewery Centre preparing to open samples of Arctic Ale with nineteenth century bottle in the centre. Behind him is a cask end from a former Bass union cask.

The arrival of the special Burton Ale at the Duke of Devonshire. In the foreground is Matthew Otley, with Geoff Mumford, Nick Otley and the author. (With kind permission of the *Burton Mail*)

The return of a Liberal government in 1905 increased the pressure on the brewers. The Licensing Bill of 1908 sought to reduce without compensation the number of pub licences, to allow local people to vote to turn their areas into 'dry' ones without licensed premises, and to ban the employment of women in pubs, which would have put an end to the much-loved British barmaid. A protest meeting filled Burton town hall and was addressed by Lord Burton in one of his last public appearances. The hostility of the government to the drinks industry encouraged the brewers in Burton to set aside their differences and competitive instincts and form an Association of Burton Brewers. The first meeting was held in John Gretton's office in 1908 and it was decided to support a mass protest meeting in London's Hyde Park on 27 September. Half a million people attended the rally, including barmaids dressed in their Sunday best. Further demonstrations were held in the Kent hop fields and in East London, which supplied most of the casual labour for hop picking every autumn. The Bill was eventually thrown out by the House of Lords but in 1909 Lloyd George, the Chancellor of the Exchequer, returned to the attack with a Budget that increased both beer duty and the cost of a public house licence. The result was a highly unpopular rise in the price of beer from 4*d* a quart [four pints] to 5*d*. The Budget was rejected by the Lords and the price of a quart returned to 4*d* but the political implications of the defeat were far-reaching, with the Parliament Act of 1911 restricting the power of the Lords to block legislation that had been approved by the elected Commons.

Under attack from the government and facing falling sales and income, the Burton brewers strove to cut their costs. As we have seen in the previous chapter, they looked to Europe and the United States for supplies of barley and hops. American hops, in particular, were of high and consistent quality due to the climate in the Pacific north-west, the main centre of the hop industry, which offers both warm temperatures and regular rainfall due to the farms' proximity to the Cascade Mountains. In England, the hop harvest was frequently ruined by sustained rather than regular rain, and attacks from pests and plant disease that were unknown in the U.S.

The brewers were ruthless in holding down their workers' pay levels. In 1910, the combined wage bill for all the brewers in the town came to £173,000 for a workforce of 3,000 weekly paid employees. Bass's total expenditure on wages and salaries amounted to just 8 per cent of the company's total costs. Wage levels in Burton had risen by no more than 50 per cent in 100 years.

To add to the brewers' woes on the sales front, exports markets were drying up as a result of European and American lager brewers attacking Africa, India and Australasia and local breweries opening up in their native countries. Bass saw its unrivalled position in the U.S. shrinking but it did receive a small boost in 1898 when a bottle of Bass Ale was sold in Dawson City in the Yukon for the high price of five dollars. The beer has survived at a temperature of 42 degrees Fahrenheit below zero and it was this ability to withstand low temperatures that encouraged Sir Ernest Shackleton to take supplies of Bass No. 1 on his Imperial Trans-Antarctic Expedition in 1914.

At home, the brewers scrapped for every account and it was a sign of the times when the great brewing empires of Allsopp and Bass desperately fought one another to supply the modest demands of the Isle of Man Steam Packet Co. In London, Bass and Worthington battled to supply pubs, offering discounts and other inducements. Bass told several bottling companies in London and East Anglia they could package only its beers, a move that was fiercely resisted by several bottlers who considered Worthington's products to be of superior quality. Bass's concerns about the state of the London market were well-founded: in 1890, the company's sales in the capital accounted for 36 per cent of its total, but a decade later that figure had fallen to 22.5 per cent. The company turned to other parts of the country. It increased sales in Liverpool and Stoke-on-Trent and opened new agencies in Belfast, Exeter and Plymouth. In spite of the difficult market conditions, Bass was one of the few British brewers to expand sales: its production fell between 1901 and 1910 but then picked up to reach 1,269,225 barrels a year on the eve of the First World War. Sixty per cent of the brewery's production was pale ale, a fact that emphasised the reverence drinkers still had for Burton beer, even if it commanded a higher price than ales from other brewing centres.

Worthington's Brewery, Burton-on-Trent   Valentines Series   43526

Worthington's Brewery, harnessing the power of the train.

Nevertheless, the troubled times had an impact even on Bass's profits, which declined from £500,000 at a year at the start of the twentieth century to less than £250,000 by 1908 and 1909. Other Burton brewers fared even less well. In 1906, Salts went into voluntary liquidation and the Burton Brewing Co. was also in difficulties and was eventually bought by Worthington. In 1888 there had been thirty-one breweries in the town, but the number fell to seventeen by 1911. Allsopp's precarious position – its sales fell by 40 per cent between 1900 and 1910 – led to protracted talks with Bass between 1910 and 1912 about the possibilities of a merger, but Bass chairman John Gretton proved a major stumbling block over the level of compensation to be paid to Allsopp's directors and shareholders. Allsopp's affairs were revived for a while in 1912 when a new chairman, J.J. Calder, arrived from the Scottish brewers, Arrols of Alloa. One of Calder's first acts was to buy the Birmingham brewery of Showell's against stiff opposition from Mitchells & Butlers and he attempted to acquire the Burton Brewery, only to lose out to Worthington. It was Worthington that went into the second decade of the new century in the strongest position. Its sales had barely slipped and its finances were sound, while other Burton brewers were either struggling to survive or were looking at depleted sales and revenues.

But the problems of the early years of the century paled into insignificance when the First World War broke out. Lloyd George, who became Minister of Munitions, now had unbridled power to shackle his old enemies, the brewers. In August 1914, the government brought in the Defence of the Realm Act, known as DORA, which gave the Home Secretary powers to control the production and supply of alcohol. This was quickly followed by the Intoxicating Liquor Act that gave magistrates the power to limit pub opening hours on the recommendation of chief constables. Permitted opening hours were cut from sixteen or seventeen hours a day – the pre-war norm – to five and a half hours during the week and five on Sundays. As a result, consumption fell dramatically. While the government rejected prohibition, it did contemplate nationalising the entire brewing industry, but backed away when the civil service produced figures showing that the cost of compensation would be around £225 million. Lloyd George was not satisfied. In a speech in Bangor in 1915 he ranted that, 'Drink is doing us more damage in the war than all the German submarines put together. We are fighting Germany, Austria and Drink; and as far as I can see the greatest of these three deadly foes is Drink'. No evidence has ever been produced to support his claim that drink and drunkenness were affecting the war effort but Lloyd George had the support of the press barons whose papers daily thundered against the threat of 'the Hun'. As a result, in June 1915 the government created the Central Control Board, which not only slashed pub opening hours but banned 'treating' – buying a drink for another person – thus putting paid during the war to the favourite British pub pastime of 'the round'. The Control Board created the State Management Scheme that took over pubs in three key areas affecting the war effort: Carlisle and Gretna Green, where a large munitions factory were based; Enfield Lock in North London, with another munitions factory; and Invergordon and Cromarty in Scotland, where a naval dockyard was based. The impact on Carlisle was especially draconian. Five local breweries were nationalised and four of them were closed while all pubs on either side of the Solway Firth were taken over by the state in an area covering 500sq miles.

The Burton brewers were left untouched as far as ownership was concerned but, in common with the rest of the industry, they felt the full force of further government measures. As a result of brewing high gravity Burton Ales and pale ales, they suffered disproportionately when excise duties were ratcheted up. One of the first acts of the government in 1914 was to increase duty from 7s 9d to 23s per standard barrel of 1,055 degrees gravity – approximately 5.5 per cent alcohol in modern measurement – with higher rates for stronger beers. Duty rates were further increased in 1917 and doubled a year later. There was no respite when the war ended, as the peace had to be paid for. Duty was raised to £3 10s in 1919 and to £5 in 1920. By 1920, duty provided £123 million for the government, compared with £13.6 million in 1913-14. Gourvish and Wilson say that in real terms, allowing for wartime inflation, the increase in duty between 1914 and 1920 was a staggering 430 per cent. Duty increases were accompanied by restrictions on production and the strength of beer. Herbert Asquith's Liberal government reduced output to some 25.3 million barrels a year, but when his government fell and was replaced by a coalition led by Lloyd George, annual beer production was pegged at just 10 million barrels. As barley could no longer be imported and grain was needed to make bread, the government introduced orders forcing brewers to reduce the strength of their beers and, as a result, to use less malting barley. In 1917, a wave of industrial unrest throughout Britain forced the Home Secretary to tell parliament that the shortage of beer had been one of the factors creating strikes. History had been turned on its head in just a few years: at the outbreak of war, Lloyd George had blamed drunkenness for injuring the war effort. Now, as the war was nearing its end, he was told by his own ministers to increase beer production to stop trade union action. His answer was to allow brewers to step up production by 20 per cent – but half of that production had to be limited to beers of no more than 1,036 degrees, around 3.5 per cent alcohol. John Gretton at Bass was active in talks between the industry and government and the rules were relaxed for some brewers of stronger beers, including the Burton brewers and Guinness in Ireland. Guinness said it was impossible to brew anything called stout at less than 1,042 degrees and the government was anxious to appease the rebellious Irish. However, in 1918, in order to direct more grain to the bread industry, the government reduced still further the proportion of weaker beer the industry could make to just

Bird's-eye view of Burton-on-Trent, 1921.

1,030 degrees (3 per cent alcohol). Much to the anger of ministers, the beer was dubbed 'Government Beer' or 'Lloyd George's Beer' and some brewers even added the terms to pump handles on pub bars. The Central Control Board quickly ruled that such descriptions could not be used at the point of dispense.

The war proved a double-edged sword for the brewing industry. The number of brewers fell by 22 per cent between 1913 and 1920, from 3,746 to 2,914. Ceaselessly attacked by the prime minister and his allies in the temperance movement, bombarded by controls and reductions in supplies, and squeezed by increases in duty, many brewers simply gave up and sold their companies. This was especially the case with companies that failed to pay a dividend to their shareholders. The war years took their toll on even the biggest brewers. Bass's barrelage fell almost by half, from 1,103,561 in 1915-16 to 518,637 in 1917-18, a decrease of 47 per cent. The strength of its beers decreased in that period from 1,061.9 degrees to 1,054.5 degrees and then fell again to 1,043.9 degrees in 1918-19. Allsopp, described by Gourvish and Wilson as 'the hapless firm', was, astonishingly, unable to pay an ordinary dividend for seventeen years, between 1901 and 1918. The writing was on the brewery wall for this former giant of Burton brewing. But in spite of all the trials and tribulations created by the war, many brewers were able to record reasonable profits. This apparent paradox is explained by the fact that costs of production fell substantially when brewers lowered the strengths of their beers, the

£100,000 worth of Oak Staves for making Casks, Bass & Co., Burton-on-Trent.

Oak staves for casks at Bass.

wage bill was reduced as a result of many workers joining the armed forces, and consumption increased once the troops returned home, even though the price of a pint had soared.

For the Burton brewers, the Victorian heyday of strong pale ales and Burton Ales was history. The burden of excise duty and consumer demand in the inter-war years for lower strength beers meant Allsopps, Bass, Worthington and the smaller producers had to concentrate on draught and bottled ales that ranged between 4 and 5 per cent alcohol. Draught Bass, the premium cask-conditioned beer, was 4.4 per cent alcohol and that figure tended to become an industry norm, though bottled beer, increasingly consumed in the comfort of middle-class homes, was higher: Worthington's White Shield, a leader in the field, measured 5.6 per cent. Between the wars, the industry was repeatedly castigated for its conservatism. The *Economist* magazine criticised the brewers for their failure to innovate and another critic denounced the industry for its 'torpor'. Not all of the criticism was well-placed. In Burton, brewing chemists worked hard to improve the quality of malts and hops. As a result of their work with farmers and maltsters, fewer ingredients were imported, which led to a decrease in costs, though grain and hops were sourced from abroad when prices were keen. Breweries were electrified, enabling beer and malt to be moved by pumps, elevators and hoists. Horse-drawn drays were replaced by lorries and vans. Union rooms were modernised, with metal replacing wood, with the exception of the union casks themselves, as these had to be fashioned from oak. But here again use was made of

British oak – wooden warships having gone out of fashion – rather than imported Polish wood.

The most controversial step in the 1920s was the move by the large London brewer Whitbread to consider replacing its naturally-conditioned bottled beer – that is, beer containing yeast that enabled conditioning in bottle – with a filtered and artificially carbonated version. An anonymous memorandum found in the papers of Sydney Neville, Whitbread's managing director, and quoted by Gourvish and Wilson, contains this fiery denunciation of Whitbread's plans:

> It is inconceivable that anyone who drinks beer thoughtfully could really prefer artificially conditioned beer. The difference is that between freshly made tea and tea made with tepid water. It is the difference between butter and margarine. It is the difference between the clear reasoning of H.G. Wells and the diatribe of an angry woman. It is the difference between real beer and sham beer... It is impossible to consider anything except naturally matured beer.

Leave aside the outdated sexism, this precisely mirrors the debates in the 1970s between the Campaign for Real Ale and giant brewers who were switching from draught cask ale to carbonated keg beer, which, CAMRA claimed, was effectively bottled beer in a bigger container. Whitbread's first small step towards chilled, filtered, pasteurised and carbonated beer was a harbinger of the upheavals that would transform brewing fifty years later and lead to a spectacular consumer revolt. In the 1920s, brewers hurried to follow Whitbread's lead. Bass and Worthington were not content to rest on the laurels of their celebrated naturally-conditioned bottled beers such as Bass Red Triangle and Worthington White Shield. Chiller units were installed in their breweries and by the late 1930s Bass Blue Triangle and Worthington's Green Shield carbonated beers accounted for around one third of the combined companies' production.

If the post-war world was a difficult one for brewers, it was doubly so for the workforce in Burton. Modernisation of plant and low consumption of beer throughout the 1920s led to a culling of brewery jobs. Even the coopers, the aristocrats of labour, who had unionised themselves in the late nineteenth century to protect their skills, were not immune to the depressed state of the economy in the 1920s. In 1922, Bass not only sacked ten of its coopers but also reduced the remaining coopers' wages on several occasions. Brewery workers' wages in the town fell from 70s a week to 50s in the early 1920s. The trades council created the Burton Unemployed Distress Fund and in 1926, during the General Strike called by the Trades Union Congress in support of striking miners, the Burton fund distributed food vouchers and paid strikers' wives 10s a week plus 4s for each child up to a maximum of 25s.

The Worthington White Shield car, used to promote the beer, on view at the National Brewery Centre in Burton.

Last of the breed in cooper's and their skills, which disappeared when metal casks replaced wood.

The economic gloom of the 1920s and the Great Depression of the 1930s led inevitably to a reduction in the number of breweries in Burton. But there were more powerful economic forces at work: even in times of economic upturn, the twentieth century was a time of concentration in industries, including brewing. The industrial revolution in the previous century had created tens of thousands of small workshops that were the driving force of the economy. But in the twentieth century, the race was on to combine and centralise production in order to protect profits and markets. Where brewing was concerned, the number of producers in Britain fell from 2,464 in 1921 to 1,502 by 1928 and then to just 840 by the outbreak of the Second World War in 1939. In Burton the sharp decline in the number of brewers was the result of both mergers and the retreat of 'foreign' companies back to their places of origin. Once it was possible to 'Burtonise' brewing water, the likes of Charrington, Boddingtons, Walkers and others saw no need to maintain two brewing centres and they returned to London, Manchester, Warrington and other centres. But the event that shook Burton's brewing roots to the core was the merger in 1926 of Bass and Worthington, for so long neighbouring but bitter competitors. It was a curious amalgamation. Kevin Hawkins, in his book on Bass Charrington, described the coming together of the two breweries as 'the biggest non-merger in the history of the brewing industry... the two companies continued to run more or less independently of each other', a situation that existed until full integration was achieved in 1955. A statement issued at the time of the merger said: 'It will be seen that the Boards of both Companies will for all practical purposes be identical, thus ensuring that in future the two companies will work together in close harmony with the result that large economies in working will be effected'. It was the 'economies of working' that were the key reason for the new arrangement. Costs of distribution were slashed, agencies were amalgamated, tied pubs sold beer from both breweries and similar brands were rationalised. For example, Bass Red Triangle and Worthington White Shield bottled beers became the same brew, although connoisseurs of both beers would continue passionately to argue the case for their favourite of 'the two'.

The most startling aspect of the merger was the dominating role played by Worthington's management. It was by far the smaller of the two companies, yet it was its senior directors who were in effective control. The reason was the decline in the influence and aspiration of the Grettons and the Ratcliffs, a situation that affected many family-owned businesses where the older generation was tired out and the younger generation – as had been the case with the Bass family – was motivated solely by how much cash it could take from the firm. Gerard Clay, a director of Bass at the time of the merger, was highly critical of his fellow directors. The Ratcliffs, he said, were almost totally apathetic while the 'Gretton command has nearly ruined this great Bass Business'. The chairman, John Gretton

– full title Colonel the Rt Hon John Gretton MP – was an active member of parliament and owned a large estate at Stapleford near Melton Mowbray. Major H.F. Gretton lived at Egginton Hall and owned Bladon House, Donington Park and a half-share in Grantham House at Cowes, Isle of Wight. Both retired at the time of the merger and took with them substantial nest-eggs from the value of their large shareholdings. Worthington, on the hand, had been led by members of the Manners family, with considerable élan, since the death of William Henry Worthington in 1894, beginning with William Posnette Manners and succeeded by his son Arthur. It was common currency in Burton that Arthur Manners had run rings round John Gretton during negotiations and emerged as the victor of the merger. As Colin Owen noted, 'to Arthur Manners the opportunity to become joint managing director of Burton's largest and most prestigious brewery must have been viewed with mouth-watering anticipation'.

Mergers and takeovers were now the order of the day. Between the late 1920s and 1930, Allsopp bought breweries in Alloa, Birmingham, Derby, Lichfield and Oxford. Ind Coope bought three breweries, including Thomas Robinson in Union Street, Burton. In 1927, Burton witnessed the end of another major brewer, Thomas Salt, when it was bought by Bass for £1,284,856. Salt had once been the fourth biggest brewery in the town but, as a result of financial difficulties since the turn of the century, it had gone into voluntary liquidations in 1906, its plant and its pubs had become rundown and the company was a long time dying. Colin Owen is blunt about the reason behind the takeover: the decision 'to purchase such a company was based purely on a desire to eliminate competition and secure retail outlets'. Two of Salt's subsidiaries, Brunt, Bucknall of Woodville and Thomas Cooper's Crescent Brewery in Burton, were sold. By the end of the 1920s the former Beeropolis was reduced to just nine breweries.

The big brewers stepped up their domination of the market with a vigorous advertising campaign. It was led by Guinness with its famous slogan 'Guinness Is Good for You' – devised by the crime writer Dorothy L. Sayers – and Bass responded with the simple slogan: 'Great Stuff, this Bass'. By 1933 Bass was spending £54,000 a year on press advertising and Worthington £34,000. The Brewers' Society, the industry umbrella organisation, came up with an even simpler slogan: 'Beer is Best'. The temperance movement responded with 'Beer is best left alone'.

The brewers with the resources to advertise their wares needed to make their voices heard as the 1930s presented them with unprecedented challenges. The 1929 stock market implosion in New York led to the Great Depression, with world-wide repercussions. While Britain fared less badly than Germany, where the collapse of the economy created fertile ground for Fascism, unemployment at home rose to 2 million in July 1930 and then to 2½ million by December that year. By 1931 the figure was hovering close to 3 million. The Labour Chancellor of the Exchequer,

Philip Snowden, increased excise duty on beer in order, he said, to provide aid for the jobless but this was seen as sophistry by the wider public as well as the brewers. The 40 per cent increase was swingeing: an average rate of £5 4s a barrel meant an increase of a penny on the price of a pint. The result was a fall in production of 8 million barrels a year between 1931 and 1933, while consumption per person fell to 104 pints a year, a figure that represented a decline of 20 per cent in a decade. In 1933, a more sensitive chancellor, Neville Chamberlain, listened to the Brewers' Society, which had energetically lobbied him, and responded by redrawing the duty scales: £1 20s per barrel of 1,027 degrees or less, plus 10d for each degree of gravity above 1,027 degrees. For brewers of 1,040 degrees beer, which had become the norm, the change meant a reduction of 35 per cent, bringing duty down below the level of the 1920s. In return, Chamberlain asked the brewers to cut the price of a pint by one penny, to increase the average gravity by 2 per cent, and to use more home-grown barley. The changes did reverse the slump in output from close to 18 million barrels in 1932/3 to 24.7 million barrels by 1938/9. But Chamberlain's largesse came too late to halt the closure of breweries that had followed Philip Snowden's earlier increases. Breweries were closing at the rate of one a month and mergers continued apace.

In Burton in 1934 the merger of Allsopp and Ind Coope put the amalgamation of Bass and Worthington in the shade. It was the biggest merger in brewing history and served to put the long-ailing Allsopp out of its financial misery. Once again, shareholders were offered the prospects of considerable savings if production and distribution were combined. The managing director of Allsopp, J.J. Calder, told a director of Ind Coope: 'You have had a difficult task building up Ind Coope's who have 1,600 Houses, and I have built up Allsopp's with 1,800 Houses. There is only a wall between our Breweries. Do you not think it would be wise for us to join forces?' The wall came down and the merger created Britain's biggest brewing group with a tied estate of 3,400 pubs. The 'considerable savings' included a further loss of jobs for Burton workers as production was rationalised.

The merger marked the fall of yet another Burton dynasty. While the name Bass was retained – even though no members of the Bass family were involved in the Bass-Worthington combine – Allsopp quietly faded from view as Ind Coope & Allsopp became eventually just Ind Coope. Samuel Allsopp, the brewer who had created the Burton trade with India and enabled the town to grow into the most important brewing centre in the world, had become just a footnote to history. Exports of Burton beer were becoming a thing of the past as well. Bass, once so famous throughout the world, saw its exports fall from 4.3 per cent of total production in 1928 to just 1.7 per cent by 1937.

A new world war threatened and brewers were understandably nervous of the impact on their business. But the Second World War proved to be different in many ways to the First. Prime Minister Winston Churchill, for a start, was not Lloyd George. A man who famously said, 'I have taken more out of alcohol than alcohol has taken out of me' was determined that both the armed forces and people manning the Home Front should not be deprived of a pint of beer. The Minister for Food, Lord Woolton, said in 1940 that while the strength of beer would have to fall to conserve raw materials and ensure the bakers were well supplied with grain, there would be no restrictions on brewing. He added: 'It is the business of the government not only to maintain the life but the morale of the country. If we are to keep up anything like approaching normal life, beer should continue to be in supply, even though it may be beer of a rather weaker variety than the connoisseur would like'. It was beer not only of a weaker kind but also with some unusual ingredients, including maize, oats and even, for a time, dried potato, while the government demanded in 1941 that hop rates should be reduced by 20 per cent in order that agricultural land could be diverted to growing fruit and vegetables.

But one aspect of the renewed hostilities with Germany didn't change: as in 1914, beer was seen as a convenient milch cow to help fund the war effort. Duty was doubled when war broke out, rose twice in 1940 and in 1942 it was increased by more than 45 per cent. There were further increases in 1943 and 1944 and in April 1944, when duty reached more than £7 a barrel; it was 486 per cent higher than before the war. The impact on the Burton brewers was especially severe and such once-famous products as Burton Ale were brewed in far smaller amounts as they commanded high levels of tax as a result of their strength. At the start of the war, production at Bass increased and in 1940 it exceeded 1 million barrels for the first time since the late 1930s. But a year later the company was forced to reduce production due to a shortage of raw material. The tax bill faced by the two Burton giants, Bass and Ind Coope, reached astronomic heights. Between 1939 and 1944, the annual amount of duty paid by Bass rose from £3.6 million to £10.7 million and in 1942/43 duty represented more than 83 per cent of the company's production costs. Nevertheless, as in 1914-18, the Burton brewers recorded reasonable profits as a result of the reduced costs of raw materials, a smaller workforce and lower investment in brewing plant and the upkeep of tied pubs. In Burton, people joined the armed forces in substantial numbers, leading to a serious shortage of labour. In place of the Norkies hired from East Anglia, who were now in uniform, the brewers brought in workers from the Irish Republic and Northern Ireland. By 1947, wages for brewery workers in the town reached an average of 78s a week, the highest since the early 1920s.

The second war was different to the first in one key regard: it was fought not only on land and sea but also in the air. Bombing had a catastrophic affect on British brewers. Thousands of pubs were razed to the ground and many experienced publicans were killed. Bombs destroyed Boddingtons brewery in

Manchester, two breweries in Sheffield were blown to bits while Barclay Perkins, Charrington, Fuller's, Manns, Taylor Walker and Young's in London were all put out of action. Ind Coope's Romford plant was attacked six times but production continued unhindered in Burton. The town escaped serious aerial attack. The only major explosion was an accident: in 1944 an arsenal of bombs stored in the cellars of former gypsum works detonated. The shockwave was recorded in Switzerland and an enormous crater was left behind. Seventy people were killed, including several Italian prisoners-of-war.

As the war ended, so too did the grip of another Burton dynasty. In 1945, Lord Gretton resigned as chairman of Bass after fifty-two years on the board and he was replaced by Arthur Manners. A new eight-man board included just one Gretton and one Ratcliff, with three Manners from the Worthington side of the business. The old order had changed again. The new management gave its workforce a day's paid holiday and a free pint of beer to celebrate victory over Germany and then faced a post-war world that would change both society and brewing out of all recognition.

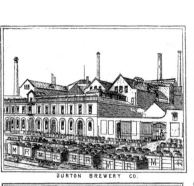

BURTON BREWERY CO.

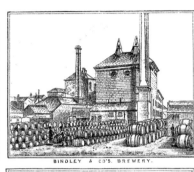

BINDLEY & CO'S. BREWERY.

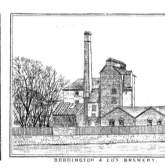

BODDINGTON & CO'S BREWERY.

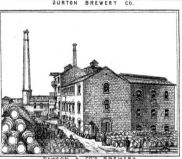

DAWSON & CO'S BREWERY.

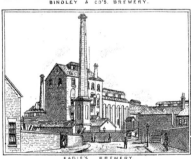

EADIE'S BREWERY

EVERSHEAD'S BREWERY.

GREEN & CLARKSON'S BREWERY.

SYKES & CO'S BREWERY.

A.B. WALKER'S BREWERY.

Staffordshire Breweries (left to right, from the top): Burton Brewery Co.; Bindley & Co.'s Brewery; Boddington & Co's Brewery; Dawson & Co.'s Brewery; Eadie's Brewery; Evershead Brewery; Green & Clarkson's Brewery; Sykes & Co.'s Brewery; A.B. Walker's Brewery.:

Chapter Seven

Into the Whirlwind

The Britain that emerged, bloodied and battered, from the Second World War was transformed in the 1960s into a vibrant new society where people had little truck with the outdated ideas and social mores of the pre-war years. But first, the British people had to struggle through a period of austerity, with war-time rationing continuing into the early 1950s. The majority Labour government led by Clement Attlee inaugurated the Welfare State and the National Health Service and also nationalised many key industries. Once again, nationalisation of the brewing industry was discussed, this time not by ministers in league with the temperance movement but by Labour MPs who had no love for the Tory-supporting 'beerage'. The costs of compensation proved yet again to outweigh the benefits of state control. The industry nevertheless was buffeted by government measures in the grim post-war years. A food crisis in 1946 meant that grain had to be directed to the bread makers and brewers were ordered to reduce their output to 85 per cent of the previous year. This was followed by a 10 per cent reduction in the strength of beer, with the minimum average set at just 1,030 degrees or 3 per cent alcohol.

There were further cuts in output the following year and excise duty was raised in both 1947 and 1948. The restrictions on strength were eventually lifted but, despite that relief, a pint of weak bitter in the late 1940s cost 1s 4d; drinkers were paying a high price for beer that was 10 per cent weaker than before the war.

In Burton, change continued at Bass. Following the departure of Lord Gretton in 1945, other members of the old guard decided to call it a day. They included Percy Ratcliff, who had been a director for forty-three years, Claude Burt, who had notched up thirty-one years and James Eadie with fourteen years' service. The grip these old timers had exercised over the company caused unease among investors and shareholders, an unease that grew as Bass's sales fell by 18 per cent between 1945 and 1954, with Worthington's bottled beers alone showing growth. Bass and Worthington were still effectively run as separate companies. Long overdue rationalisation was repeatedly put off. Finally even Arthur Manners was persuaded to step down and was replaced by an outsider, Sir James Grigg, in 1953. The *Economist* newspaper clearly had Bass in its sights in 1964 when it launched a stinging attack on the beerage: 'Traditionalist, paternalistic, inbred, secretive – Britain's brewing industry slumbered through the 1950s, hogging over £1,000 million of capital.' The industry was, the *Economist* said in a pithy phrase, 'a picturesque dinosaur.'

Change, however, was underway that would bring the dinosaur back to life. Following the war, there was great consumer resistance to the quality of draught beer served in pubs. The poor quality was the result of the low strength permitted by the government, which meant beer deteriorated quickly in cask. The problem was compounded by the fact that many experienced publicans had been killed during the war, either in the armed services or as a result of bombing at home. New and inexperienced publicans weren't trained in the arcane rituals of 'tapping and spiling' casks and allowing beer to settle until clear of sediment. All too often a pub pint was expensive, weak and cloudy. The result was a switch by consumers to the certainties of bottled beer, especially the filtered and carbonated versions pioneered by Whitbread before the war. Bottled beer also had the important advantage of being stronger than draught. There was such a surge in the sales of bottled beer that by 1959 it accounted for 36 per cent of total beer production. The change was of great benefit to the Burton brewers Ind Coope in particular, whose Double Diamond pale ale became one of the biggest-selling brands. Worthington's traditional bottled beers held up well but the group also saw growth in demand for its carbonated versions, which were brewed by Bass as the Worthington plant lacked the equipment to filter, pasteurise and carbonate beer.

Sales of draught beer in pubs started to recover once the post-war recession and the rationing of ingredients ended. The brewers could have put great effort in to boosting the fortunes of traditional ale but several major producers were determined to move to a different type of draught beer. The reasoning was simple: if consumers enjoyed carbonated bottled beer then why not serve chilled and filtered beer on draught as well, especially as filtered beer had – to use a new buzz term of the time – a longer 'shelf life'?

In the late 1930s, the London brewer Watney had experimented with draught beer that was pasteurised and then pumped into a sealed metal canister and impregnated with carbon dioxide. As it was sterile beer, it would stay in drinkable condition for several months. The experimental beer was meant for troops in India – no IPA for them – but some was diverted to an outpost of the empire, the East Sheen Tennis Club in Surrey, where members complained that cask ale consumed mainly at weekends was often in poor condition. The new beer was named Red Barrel and its impact after the war helped change brewing out of all recognition.

The switch to container beer was slow at first as a result of the post-war recession, shortage of raw materials and the urgent need for brewers to improve their tied estates. But as economic problems eased, the large regional brewer J.W. Green of Luton entered the canister market in 1955 with a beer called Flowers Keg; Flowers was a brewery in Stratford-upon-Avon that had been taken over by Greens, complete with its logo depicting William Shakespeare. Keg was the name given to the metal container that held the beer: it was dubbed a 'sealed dustbin' by the Campaign for Real Ale in the 1970s. The success of Flowers Keg in the large Green's tied estate prompted other brewers to join the rush to carbonated beer. In several cases, existing bottled and cask ales were turned into keg on the grounds that consumers were already familiar with the brand names. Flowers Keg was a processed version of the existing cask ale, Flowers Original. In Burton, Ind Coope took its best-selling bottled pale ale, Double Diamond, and reduced it from 4.7 per cent to 3.8 for the keg version. Bass followed a similar path to Greens by transforming Worthington E from cask to keg. To the relief of beer connoisseurs, Draught Bass was left in traditional form, but keg – which eventually also embraced the first attempts at British lager – rolled on like a brewing tsunami, sweeping away smaller breweries and brands that stood in its path. The launch of Flowers Keg coincided with the arrival of commercial television; the first beer to appear on ITV was Watney's Red Barrel and it was soon followed by two Burton brands, Double Diamond – which, the jingle assured us, Works Wonders – and Worthington E. The Worthington promotion appealed, rather curiously given the modern nature of the beer, to nostalgia. Edwardian men and women were seen cycling to idyllic country pubs, trilling the old music hall song 'Daisy, Daisy, give me your answer, do'. In 1977, according to the Media Expenditure Analysis, Bass spent £310,000 promoting Worthington on TV and in the media. Draught Bass, on the other hand, had to make do with leaflets in pubs urging drinkers to 'ask for cask'.

The total advertising budget for all Britain's brewers in 1977 was £70 million and the majority of that sum was devoted to keg beer and lager. In 1959, keg beer accounted for just 1 per cent of beer sales. By 1965 it had grown to 7 per cent, by 1971 18 per cent. Just five years later, keg controlled 63 per cent of beer production. The brewers claimed they were merely bowing to demand by introducing keg beer, a claim rebutted by Graham Bannock in 1971 in his book *The Juggernauts*: 'More probably it [keg beer] simply reflects the exercise of marketing power... Without tied sales outlets and without heavy selective advertising it is most unlikely that keg beers could have been introduced on anything like the scale so far achieved. As it is, the Juggernaut brewers will soon be in a position to abolish cask beer altogether, although it will no doubt be attributed to the power of the market'.

Early twentieth century – the internal combustion engine replaced the train to deliver beer. (On view at the National Brewery Centre.)

The impact on the industry was cataclysmic. Smaller brewers who were unable to afford the investment needed to produce keg – metal containers, chiller, filtration and pasteurisation units, let alone the ability to spend on advertising – pulled down the shutters. If they owned pubs, they took the keg beers offered by bigger brewers. Handpumps and beer engines needed to serve cask beer disappeared like the snows of winter. Between 1940 and 1950 the number of breweries in Britain fell by a third, from 840 to 567, before the impact of keg beer was felt. By 1980, only eighty-one breweries were left. The repercussions in Burton were evident to the eye: the ancient skills of coopers was swept away as metal casks and kegs replaced wood, and the vast yards used to store wooden casks became derelict. Giant conical fermenters started to dominate the skyline outside breweries while all the new trappings of keg beer production were installed inside them. By the mid-1950s, the breweries' rail systems were torn up as the companies switched from trains to trucks to deliver beer by road. British Rail refused to meet Bass's request for a freight depot in the town and instead increased charges for transporting beer. As a result, Bass and the other Burton brewers moved to road deliveries, a trend that accelerated as a new motorway system started to develop.

In 1955, Bass and Worthington were at long last fully integrated as one company. The downside of the amalgamation was a further loss of jobs. Bass Middle Brewery closed in 1957 and the Worthington plant was shut eight years later. Fortunately the large areas of land vacated by the brewers enabled a number of engineering firms to set up in business in the town and they offered pay rates that were substantially better than those paid by the breweries. The Marmite factory, based in Cross Street, moved to new and bigger premises in 1961 that were conveniently close to Marston's brewery, where it was assured of regular supplies of excess yeast.

But 1961 was a year that heralded changes in Burton that were rather more momentous than a new factory geared to yeast extract. In March, Ind Coope merged with Ansells of Birmingham and Tetley Walker in Leeds to form ICTA, which immediately became the biggest brewing group in Britain, with 8,000 pubs and breweries strategically placed in the south, centre and north of Britain, with a further brewery in Alloa, Scotland, that concentrated on lager. In July, Bass merged with the large Mitchells & Butlers brewery in Birmingham and overnight became the third biggest brewer behind ICTA – renamed Allied Breweries in 1962 – and Guinness. Driving the mergers was the whirlwind of activity generated by an outsider, E.P.Taylor, from Canada. E.P. stood for Edward Plunket, but he was known to his friends as Eddie. Taylor was an industrialist who had moved into brewing in Canada and the United States in the 1930s. He bought a brand of lager with the unappetising name of Carling Black Label Rice Beer and promptly and wisely dropped the word rice. By the 1950s, Taylor's Canadian Breweries dominated his homeland and he was also selling beer in the northern-most states of the U.S. But Canada is a large country with a small population while there were major barriers to expansion in the U.S. in the form of the big three brewing giants Anheuser-Busch, Coors and Miller.Taylor looked to Britain, which was the opposite of Canada: a small country with a large beer-drinking population.To his astonishment, the Brits were not drinking lager and he planned to change that.

Taylor was a noisy, bustling businessman, at odds with the gentlemen of the British beerage with their club culture and behind-the-arras style of conducting their affairs. And Taylor frightened the life out of them: they had never been confronted by this type of aggressive North American behaviour before. One brewery company director, quoted by Gourvish and Wilson, said Taylor 'had been

Left to right: R.J.A.P. Charrington, E.P. Taylor and Sir Alan Walker in the talks that created Bass Charrington.

driving round the United Kingdom and bursting upon startled directors… with only the slimmest of introductions, suggesting mergers with the eloquence of a carbon paper salesman'. In short, Taylor was not a gentleman.

In order to turn Carling into a national brand, Taylor needed pubs and breweries. He moved liked lightning. In just ten months in 1960, he bought twelve breweries in Scotland and the north of England. A further four breweries were added the following year to form a new company, Northern United. Taylor's great coup that year was to convince one of the biggest and most famous London brewers, Charrington, to join his group, which was renamed Charrington United. In 1963 he bought Scotland's best-known lager brewery, Tennents, and then paused for three years before his most audacious bid. Following protracted talks, he persuaded Bass, Mitchells & Butlers to join his group, turning it into Bass Charrington. In less than a decade – and with the further addition of Hancock's in Cardiff, Stones in Sheffield and Joules of Stone, Staffordshire – Taylor had created the biggest brewing group in Britain, and controlled 20 per cent of the industry's annual production; he owned 11,000 pubs and had an annual turnover of £900 million. At the centre of this giant spider's web was Bass in Burton, once a respected, family-owned business but now transformed into a behemoth with a decreasing interest in its brewing heritage. Eddie Taylor, flush with money and success, retired to the Caribbean where he owned a string of racehorses, the only known interest he shared with the British beerage.

In other parts of the industry, further mergers were transforming brewing. In London, takeovers created Watney Mann & Truman, which also included Wilson's of Manchester and Webster's of Halifax. The breweries were absorbed into the Grand Metropolitan leisure group in 1971. Courage, also in London, merged with its near neighbour, Barclay Perkins, and also with Simonds of Reading and then John Smith's in Tadcaster. The group was taken over by Imperial Tobacco. Between 1961 and 1968, Whitbread bought no fewer than twenty-two regional and local breweries and, at the same time, acquired 9,000 pubs. In 1960 Scottish Brewers – itself a merger between McEwan and Younger – merged with Newcastle Breweries to create Scottish & Newcastle. The result was the emergence of what was called the Big Six: Allied, Bass, Courage, Watney, Whitbread and S&N – who produced 80 per cent of the country's beer, most of it in the form of keg beer and lager.

The reasons for what Gourvish and Wilson called 'mergia mania' were complex. The City of London was awash with cash and predators like the property tycoon Charles Clore were on the lookout for acquisitions. Breweries were a prime target as they owned between them more than 70,000 licensed premises, most of them seriously under-valued. Clore made an unsuccessful bid for Watney Mann and drove the brewing group into the arms of Maxwell Joseph's Grand Metropolitan, which already owned Truman's. The brewing subsidiary was part of a vast conglomerate that had an arrangement with Carlsberg for lager and also sold wine, spirits, cider and Coca-Cola, all of which could be sold through the brewing division's 7,000 pubs. The fact that Grand Met also owned Chef & Brewer, Berni Inns and Schooner Inns was significant, for brewers were now firmly part of what was dubbed 'the leisure industry' in which eating-out became an important attraction.

Britain was visibly a different society in the Swinging Sixties. The population was booming, young working-class people were kicking down class barriers that stood in their way, while middle-class women were for the first time going to pubs in growing numbers. The 'baby boomers' were drinking more alcohol: between 1955 and 1979, wine, spirits and cider grew by 7.4, 5.2 and 4.3 per cent respectively. Beer consumption was on the increase, too. In the 1950s, beer production stubbornly stuck at 25 million barrels a year but then rose from 24.6 million barrels in 1958 to 42.1 million in 1979, an increase of 71 per cent. The generation that was drinking more alcohol and eating out in pubs was also going abroad on package holidays and coming across a new type of beer called lager.

In Burton, before Bass joined Taylor's consortium to form Bass Charrington, it had first merged with Mitchells & Butlers of Birmingham. This was a case of history repeating itself: as with the Worthington merger in the 1920s, it was a smaller, more vigorous company swallowing the stagnating Burton giant. Alan Walker, later Sir Alan, who became chairman of Mitchells & Butlers in 1956, was an industrialist with no previous knowledge of brewing but who introduced a modern dynamism to the Birmingham firm, with a fresh approach to marketing and investment. M&B enjoyed a major presence in the West Midlands that was based on a large tied trade. Bass, on the other hand, was still mainly a free-trade brewer. The attraction to Walker was Bass's national sales and the prestige of its brands. It was Walker who approached Sir James Grigg, his opposite number at Bass, with the notion of a merger. Grigg, no doubt to Walker's surprise, rapidly agreed. The contract was signed in July 1961, with Walker as chief executive and Grigg as chairman. Merger is a misnomer: in effect, Bass became a subsidiary of M&B, with M&B shareholders receiving two shares in the new company for every one held. In 1963, when Sir James Grigg died, Walker took full control and while the name Bass fronted the new company, as it would do when it became Bass Charrington, in effect the brewery founded by William Bass and continued by his sons and the Grettons and Ratcliffs, ceased to exist. In 1963, Walker rubbed salt in the wound by moving the administrative headquarters of the business to Birmingham. A survey in 1961 showed that Bass and Worthington brewed around 1.5 million barrels a year, of which 71.5 per cent was in draught form. While Worthington E was a leading national brand, sales of cask Draught Bass had held up well under the keg onslaught.

Walker was determined to cut costs in order to boost profits and a ruthless policy of redundancies was carried out in Burton. Malting in particular became heavily mechanised, though Bass continued to supply 70 per cent of the group's requirements. In 1965, as noted above, the Worthington Brewery closed and work started on a new No. 1 plant. It came on stream in 1968 with an annual capacity of 400,000 barrels. The following year, the Bass Old Brewery on High Street closed, putting an end to almost two centuries of brewing. The New Brewery followed a similar fate in 1975 while No. 1 was extended to have an annual capacity of 1½ million barrels. The effect of mechanisation of all levels of beer production was reflected in employment figures. In 1902 Bass had employed a total of 3,500 men and boys, including clerical staff. By 1980 the figure had fallen to just 940.

The biggest changes, however, were outside Burton. The group spent most of the 1970s building an enormous new brewery at Runcorn in Cheshire capable of producing 2½ million barrels a year of keg, canned beer and lager. Runcorn led to a cull of older breweries, including Charrington in East London. In 1979 Charrington disappeared from the group name, which became Bass Brewers. In the 1980s, when Bass advertised Charrington IPA as the most popular real ale in London, it failed to point out that the beer had been moved first to M&B's Springfield subsidiary in Wolverhampton and, when that site closed, moved again to M&B's main plant at Cape Hill in Birmingham. As a sign of the times, Alan Walker busily built a hotels division. In 1969, a new subsidiary, Crest Hotel, was created with 120 outlets. This was followed in 1973 with the acquisition of 27 motels from Esso, 18 of which were in mainland Europe. Walker then moved further into the leisure industry by buying Pontin's resorts and Holiday Club International. This flirtation with hotels would prove to be Bass's nemesis at the turn of the century.

Allied Breweries, including Ind Coope, witnessed changes that were equally eventful and at times bizarre. At first the group recorded healthy improvements in sales and profits: production rose by 27 per cent between 1960 and 1967 while profits increased by 19 per cent, from £12.7 million in 1960 to £20.3 million in 1967. But in common with other Big Six brewers, it was restless for acquisitions outside brewing. In 1968, Allied bought Showerings and Whiteways, producers of wine and cider. Whiteways had developed the fizzy perry drink Babycham, which was enormously popular in the 1950s and '60s and was the first alcoholic drink to be advertised on commercial television. Allied strengthened its beer side by buying two Dutch breweries, Breda and Oranjeboom, and then held prolonged talks with the global giant Unilever with a view to a merger. Allied thought its future lay in lager brewing. It had the leading keg ale Double Diamond but moved into lager with Ind Coope Long Life and Skol. Skol, with its mock-Scandinavian name based on the word for a toast – skål – was for a time promoted with the aid of the cartoon Viking character Hagar the Horrible, which presented critics of the beer with an open goal to shoot at. Allied saw Skol as a potential global brand and in 1964 it created a company called Skol International that included Labatt of Canada, Pripps in Sweden and Unibra in Belgium. A tie-up with Unilever would, Allied's directors thought, give its lagers world-wide support and promotion. But the proposed merger was referred to the Monopolies Commission and both Allied and Unilever went cold on the plan. The problem for Allied was a simple one: Long Life was not a good beer and was probably not a lager at all but just pale ale served cold, while Skol, when it competed in countries with a long lager tradition, was also found wanting. Long Life was rapidly withdrawn as a draught beer and became a cheap supermarket canned product, while Skol never achieved its potential.

Allied remained desperate to join a global group and in 1978 it shocked the City by merging with J. Lyons, which had international credentials but in a field far removed from beer: cakes, biscuits, coffee and ice cream. To outside observers, it looked as though Allied Breweries, now Allied-Lyons, was losing its way, but the directors of the new group took comfort from the fact that it was now on a par with Grand Metropolitan on the world stage.

Bass was also moving into lager production. Courtesy of Eddie Taylor, it owned the major lager brand, Carling, and in 1961 joined the Harp Lager consortium created by Guinness that also included Courage, Barclays and Scottish & Newcastle. When Harp was turned into a draught product it quickly became the leading lager brand in Britain, with a 25 per cent share of the sector. Both Allied and Bass were desperate to build a strong lager portfolio as keg beer went into sharp decline. Sales of Double Diamond slumped catastrophically by 60 per cent between 1971 and 1978, with beer's contribution to overall Allied profits falling from 75 to 57 per cent, and its share of the British beer market down from 15.5 to 14 per cent. Double Diamond was not the only keg beer in free-fall. Worthington E was also in sharp decline but the biggest loser was Watney: it revamped Red Barrel as Red in 1971 and, backed by a risible advertising campaign called the Red Revolution – with lookalikes of Chairman Mao, Nikita Khrushchev and Fidel Castro the unlikely recipients of pints of the beer – saw sales fall off the cliff. The beer was withdrawn in 1979.

The year 1971 was a fateful one. Four young men, Michael Hardman, Graham Lees, Bill Mellor and Jim Makin, were so profoundly dissatisfied with the quality of beer in pubs that they set up the Campaign for the Revitalisation of Ale, soon changed to the more manageable Campaign for Real Ale – or CAMRA for short. Hardman, Lees and Mellor were journalists and were adept at attracting publicity for their cause. Their first conference was attended by only thirty people, but when the group was publicised in the *Guardian* thousands rushed to join, and offices and staff were hired to cope with the rising membership. A beer festival in 1975 in

London's Covent Garden attracted 40,000 drinkers. By 1976, CAMRA had 29,000 members and its success proved just how badly the big brewers had misread the market. As Graham Bannock had observed in his book *The Juggernauts*, keg beer had been the triumph of marketing over genuine demand and there were still millions of drinkers who preferred the full flavours of natural cask ale. Regional and family brewers who had survived the onslaught of mergers and the switch to keg could now put their heads above the parapet and start to promote cask beer with enthusiasm. In Burton, both Bass and Ind Coope had to rekindle an interest in cask. It was easier for Bass than its rival, as it had never abandoned Draught Bass, merely under-promoted it. Ind Coope re-entry into the cask market took everyone by surprise, including the brewery. In 1976, it invited journalists to Burton for the launch of Draught Burton Ale, a 4.8 per cent beer that was a cask version of bottled Double Diamond rather than a true Burton. Ind Coope expected the beer to be sold in a small number of its tied pubs but the astonishing demand for the beer, despite limited promotion, forced the brewery to extend the supply to thousands of pubs. Gaskell & Chambers in Birmingham, the country's biggest manufacturer of beer engines and hand pumps, was forced to put its staff on permanent overtime to cope with the clamour for dispense equipment from publicans who had sold only pressurised keg for years.

The success of CAMRA was two-fold: it secured the future of cask beer, and it stopped further takeovers and mergers that put an end to the carnage of the 1960s and '70s, when the total number of beers brewed in Britain fall by half, from 3,000 to less than 1,500. But CAMRA couldn't stop the onward march of lager, a style that was dominated by the likes of Allied, Bass and the other Big Six brewers who alone had the funds to invest in the different technology required to brew lager. In 1971, lager accounted for just 7 per cent of beer sales. Five years later, lager had overtaken bitter. Ten years on, lager sales reached 43.5 per cent of total beer sales and by 1989 it had become the dominant style, with 50.3 per cent of sales. The lager brewers were aided by a series of blisteringly hot summers in the 1970s, 1976 in particular, that provided free advertising for 'cold beer'. The hot weather encouraged the brewers to increase their promotions for lager. The reason was simple: British lager was weak, often pathetically so, and as a result attracted lower rates of duty than bitter. But it was priced as a premium product and as a result was immensely profitable for the brewers, five times more profitable than bitter. It was the profitability of lager that encouraged the brewers to spend vast sums promoting it. In 1967, the industry spent just £286,000 advertising lager. By 1974 the lager budget had increased to £3.2 million. In 1977, out of £20.32 million spent on total beer advertising, £9.8 million was devoted to lager. Spending on lager rose by 49 per cent in 1976 and 1977, while the Harp group, of which Bass was a member, increased spending by 66 per cent.

Bass's addiction to lager had seen the group add the Danish beer Tuborg to its range. The Bass version had an original gravity of 1,030 degrees – one degree less and it would have been classified as 'near beer' – but it sold in 1978 for 39*d* a pint. The group's M&B Mild, brewed in Birmingham, had an OG of 1,034 yet sold for 28*d* a pint, eleven pence cheaper. Allied's Skol had an OG of 1,037 and sold for 36½*d*. Ind Coope Bitter had an identical strength but sold for 30*d* a pint. Skol Special was 1,045 degrees and cost 41*d* a pint while Ind Coope Draught Burton Ale was two degrees stronger at 1,047 – yet cost 37*d* a pint. The brewers claimed it cost more to make lager but independent analysts found that longer lagering [maturation] time and investment in lager technology added just one penny to the price of a pint. And lagering times were brief. In 1976, when lager sales soared as the sun beat down, Whitbread was asked if it stored its version of Heineken (1,036 OG) in the true Continental fashion. 'Yes,' a spokesman replied, 'for at least a week'. A month would be the minimum time in Europe and in some cases is as long as three months. Most European lagers are around 5 per cent alcohol and in 1976 a German newspaper, the *Suddeutsche Zeitung* in Munich, described British lager as fit only for 'refined ladies, people with digestive ailments, tourists and other weaklings'.

The dominance of the Big Six became a cause for concern. Independent brewers complained it was difficult for them to compete on equal terms with giant brewers who not only owned 76 per cent of the country's pubs but also tied great swathes of the so-called free trade though loans and discounts. Between 1966 and 1986 there were no fewer than fifteen reports into the state of the industry, including an investigation in 1969 by the Monopolies Commission that found the tied house system to be anti-competitive. All the reports mouldered on civil servants' shelves. Nothing was done to tackle the power of the Big Six until Margaret Thatcher arrived in Downing Street in 1979. Thatcher and her doctrine of monetarism proved a disaster for the brewing industry and would lead eventually to the disappearance of both Bass and Ind Coope in Burton. Beer sales were on the increase in 1979 but the first of several recessions during her premiership sent sales into a long, downward spiral. One of the enduring images of the Thatcher years shows her standing on a large derelict plot of land in northern England that had once housed factories. The destruction of the country's manufacturing base – today it accounts for just 13 per cent of Gross National Product – meant there were far fewer throats that needed to be refreshed after eight hours digging coal or making steel and cars. Thatcher's economic mission seriously weakened brewing but she prepared a political attack as well. As the daughter of a small shopkeeper in Grantham, she had no time for 'old money' and that visceral dislike included the Beerage, where many senior directors owed their positions not to hard work but inheritance. In her famous phrase, they were 'not one of us'. The

renamed Monopolies and Mergers Commission was called in to investigate and
in 1989 it delivered a stinging rebuke to the Big Six in a 500-page report called
The Supply of Beer. Its conclusions underscored the criticisms from CAMRA and
independent brewers: the price of beer had risen too far; the high price of lager
was not justified by the cost of producing it; and consumer choice was restricted
because big brewers refused to stock beer from smaller producers in both the tied
and free trade.

The MMC concluded:

> A complex monopoly situation exists in favour of the brewers with tied estates
> and loan ties... we believe that the complex monopoly has enabled brewers with
> tied estates to frustrate the growth of brewers without tied estates; to do the same
> to independent wholesalers and manufacturers of cider and soft drinks; to keep
> tenants in a poor bargaining position; and to stop a strong independent sector
> emerging to challenge them at the retail level. We believe also that, over time, the
> monopoly has served to keep the bigger brewers big and the smaller brewers small.

The report rejected total abolition of the tie as it would damage the interests of
small brewers, but the MMC recommended that the national brewers – the Big
Six – could each own not more that 2,000 on-licensed premises, requiring them to
sell-off some 22,000 pubs and hotels. The commission also called for the elimination
of all loan ties and the right of any pub tenant to buy a minimum of one draught
beer free of the tie. Thatcher's Trade and Industry Secretary Lord Young said he was
'minded' to implement the recommendations, but the Beer Orders that followed
were something of a compromise. This was the result of pressure from many Tory
backbenchers whose constituency associations received generous financial support
from brewers. Young said that from 1 May 1990 the Big Six had two years to remove
the tie completely from half their pubs – some 11,000 – while the remaining 20,000
pubs had to be allowed to take one 'guest beer'. Following intense lobbying by
CAMRA, it was decided the guest beer had to be a cask ale to prevent pubs being
swamped by heavily-advertised keg beers and lagers. But even this compromise
was too much for the national brewers. If they couldn't brew beer and tie pubs,
their whole monopolistic *raison d'être* collapsed. A flurry of activity throughout the
1990s saw the Big Six debating first whether to either brew beer or own pubs and
eventually deciding to do neither. The rush to get out of brewing started in 1991
when Grand Metropolitan sold its Watney's brewing subsidiary to Courage, which
was now owned by Elders IXL/Foster's of Australia. In the same year, Allied Lyons
announced it would run all its breweries, including Ind Coope, as a joint venture
with Carlsberg of Denmark, to be known as Carlsberg-Tetley, while ownership of
Allied's pubs would be run by a new subsidiary Allied Retail. This arrangement was

short-lived. In 1994, Allied Lyons merged with Pedro Domecq and became Allied Domecq. The overseas wine side of the new group had no interest in British brewing. Ind Coope Romford closed in 1997 (Ansells in Birmingham had shut down long before, in 1981) and in 1996 sold its share of Carlsberg-Tetley to Bass. When the sale was blocked by the competition authorities, Carlsberg-Tetley was left as the sole owner of what was left of the former Allied Breweries. Bass was allowed to buy Ind Coope's Burton plant in 1997, but the last remaining big brewer in the town was preparing its own exit from beer making, preferring to concentrate on Holiday Inns and other hotel interests.

In 2000, Whitbread announced it would concentrate on hotels, health clubs and other leisure activities. It sold its breweries for £400 million to the Belgian group Interbrew, best-known for Stella Artois lager, which Whitbread had brewed under licence for many years. Soon afterwards, Interbrew said it would add Bass's breweries at a cost of £2.3 billion. As Interbrew would account for more than 30 per cent of the entire British beer market – in breach of competition guidelines – and would own two leading lager brands, Carling and Stella, it was told by the Department of Trade and Industry it could buy Whitbread's business but not Bass's as well. After an appeal, Interbrew was left with Tennent's in Scotland, the Ulster Brewery in Northern Ireland and some of Bass's brands, including Draught Bass, but the most profitable part of Bass Brewer's operation, the Burton breweries, had to go. On 24 December 2001, Interbrew gave a large Christmas present to the giant American brewer Coors: in return for £1.2 billion, Coors could have the Burton business and Britain's biggest beer brand, Carling.

Following twenty years of turbulence, at the end of the first decade of the new century the brewing industry and pub retailing had changed out of all recognition. But, despite or as a result of, the Beer Orders back in 1989/90, the consumer was no better served. In place of national brewers, three large non-brewing property companies own more than half the country's pubs. They are Enterprise Inns, Punch Taverns and – with ten out of ten marks for cynicism – Mitchells & Butlers. M&B was created from the ashes of Bass's pub estate and was given the name even though the Birmingham brewery closed in 2002. As for brewing, the national giants are now all foreign owned: Scottish & Newcastle by Heineken, Bass and Ind Coope by Molson Coors (Coors of the U.S. having merged with Molson of Canada), Tetley by Carlsberg, and Whitbread by what is now the world's biggest brewer, A-B InBev. First Interbrew of Belgium merged with Ambev of Brazil to form InBev and then bought the biggest American brewer Anheuser-Busch (owner of Budweiser) to form A-B InBev.

The sad epitaph for brewing in central Burton is that in 2010 A-B InBev said it was putting up for sale four cask beers previously owned by Bass and Whitbread. They are Draught Bass, Boddingtons Bitter, Flower's Original and Flower's IPA.

The cost is £15 million. A–B InBev says it has no interest in such 'low volume' brands. Draught Bass was once worth close to 1 million barrels a year but, under-promoted for decades, production has declined to around 35,000 barrels. To date, there have been no takers for the beers, mainly as a result of A–B InBev's determination to retain ownership of the trademarks for the brands, including the historic Bass Red Triangle.

A–B InBev doesn't brew such a 'low volume' beer as Draught Bass. This has been handed to Marston's in Burton. As we shall now see, there is still one major brewer left in the town with a commitment to heritage and tradition.

Chapter Eight

KEEPING THE FAITH

At Marston's they call the union rooms, with due reverence, the 'Cathedrals of Brewing'. It's the last brewery to use a system that singled out Burton in the nineteenth century as the citadel of pale ale. The unions cleanse fermenting beer of yeast but, along with the Trent Valley's singular waters, also help create a unique aroma and flavour: a powerful waft of sulphur that gives way to a complex palate of biscuity malt, spicy hops and a hint of tart fruit. While Bass's old union sets now languish in a car park alongside the National Brewery Centre, Marston's remains true to a method of fermentation that it believes is critical to producing true Burton pale ale. The unions survive at Marston's not for reasons of nostalgia – they are expensive to maintain, requiring top-quality oak and resident coopers to repair the casks – but because they create fine beer and give the brewery its now unique and iconic status.

In common with most of the Burton companies, Marston's origins were humble. At the close of the eighteenth century, Edward Marston, a cork cutter from Nottingham, married Ann Hackett from Burton and he decided to try his hand at brewing by taking over the Cock Inn in the High Street at Uttoxeter, which had a small brewhouse attached. Edward had no head for business and by 1805 he was bankrupt. His son John fared better and by 1818 he was running a successful business in Wood Street, off Anderstaff Lane, Burton, as a grocer, tea dealer, and rag, horsehair and skin merchant. (The skin was animal, not human!) In 1825, John expanded into malting, a profitable trade in the town, and he bought the malt house of Coat's brewery on the corner of Horninglow Road and Patch Lane, close to the Trent & Mersey Canal. At that time, Horninglow was a suburb of Burton and it didn't officially become part of the town until a modern borough was formed late in the nineteenth century. By 1834, John was brewing as well as malting, no doubt encouraged by the 1830 Beer Act that allowed house owners to make beer if they paid two guineas a year for a licence.

When John died in 1846, at the age of sixty-two, he was a wealthy man with a flourishing brewery. He had three sons: Henry, John Hackett and William. Henry and William worked for the brewery but John Hackett Marston became the sole owner of the company, which he expanded four times; he also added several pubs. When further expansion was planned in 1879, John Hackett looked for business partners and he joined forces with William Wayte and Richard Eddie. In the same year the company, following in the footsteps of Bass and the other Burton brewers, registered its trademark of three barrels.

In 1888, John Hackett Marston was once again the sole owner of the brewery. He never married and when he retired he sold the business to Henry Emmanuel Sugden and ended the Marston's connection, though – as with Bass – the family name continued to front the brewery. Sugden had been a partner in Joseph Nunneley's brewery in Bridge Street. When Nunneley's became a limited company, Sugden decided to branch out on his own. He bought Marston's and added a number of pubs. In 1889, Alfred Barnard, in his compendious work *Noted Breweries of Great Britain and Ireland*, described Marston's as a substantial and vigorous business producing mild, pale ale and Burton Ale. 'Not long since the brewery came into the possession of Mr H.E. Sugden, late of the firm of Nunneley & Co, Burton, who is now the sole proprietor. On making the object of our visit known to this gentleman, he introduced us to Mr Cook, his head brewer, by whom we were conducted through the premises.' It seems scarcely credible that Barnard turned up unannounced and without an appointment, and then took up several hours of the head brewer's day. Nevertheless, with his entourage of note takers and sketchers, he was shown round the maltings, the kilns, the stables, the wells and the brewhouse. Thanks to Barnard, we have a graphic account of Marston's fermenting regime that, while on a different site, hardly differs today:

We inspected the two open coolers and two vertical refrigerators, and then descended to the fermenting room underneath. It contains seven fermenting squares the largest of which holds 80 barrels, and several other vessels. The ground floor is used as a fining house, for the firm brew porter as well as ale, when required for supplying their own public houses. Again crossing the yard, we entered a detached building nearly 100ft in length, the upper storey of which is devoted to the union rooms, and contains 80 union casks fitted with attemperators [coolers] and overhead yeast troughs. The entire ground floor is utilised as racking rooms and ale cellars, and will hold nearly 1,000 casks.

Barnard concluded his visit by noting that 'nearly 50 persons are employed upon the premises, and the ales are principally sold in the locality and the Midland Counties.' In 1890, Sugden merged with Yeomans Blue Posts Inn and Brewery and started a series of moves that would turn it, by the end of the century, into an even more impressive business than the one recorded by Barnard. John Yeomans was a long-standing Burton brewing company but in 1890 it was inherited by Alfred Yeomans, who had no interest in the business and put the brewery, pubs and maltings up for sale. When they failed to reach his asking price, he merged instead with Marston's. A year later, Sugden was on the move again and bought the Bowler family's Anchor Inn and Brewery in New Street, Burton. The demand for his Burton Ale and pale ale was so great that he was forced to reopen Yeomans for a while in order to brew sufficient beer. Clearly further expansion was needed – and so was capital. In 1890, Marston's became a limited company, and a share issue in 1896 raised £100,000. Sugden used some of the cash to add new pubs, building an estate of ninety-nine houses. He followed two years later with an audacious merger with John Thompson & Son's Horninglow Street Brewery – audacious because, as in the manner of Worthington's and Mitchells & Butler's mergers with Bass, it was a case of the smaller company swallowing the bigger one. Thompsons dated from 1765 when brewing took place at the Bear Inn, Horninglow Street. The family became 'common brewers' in 1846 and the business was registered in 1887. By the time of the merger, Thompson owned two breweries and a sizeable pub estate. The amalgamation more than doubled the size of the company and bigger premises were needed to cope with the number of vessels required to keep pace with demand from both a substantial tied estate and the free trade. The new board of directors for J. Marston, Thompson & Son Ltd included Frederick Hurdle as chairman. Hurdle was from East Anglia, where he had owned a brewery, and he brought with him useful knowledge of the best suppliers of malting barley from the region as well as good contacts among London publicans and agencies. The Hurdles would continue to play a leading role in Marston's until 1999.

In 1898 the new company took what seemed a dangerous gamble: it leased the large Albion Brewery in Shobnall Road. It had been owned by the Albion Brewery Co. for just one year and the site was previously the Burton base for the London firm Mann, Crossman & Paulin. As we have seen earlier, MCP was just one of several brewers from London that had rushed to Burton in the nineteenth century to use the Trent Valley waters to fashion their interpretations of pale ale. MCP built a 30-acre site with not only a brewery but also a model village for its workers and even a small church. Marston's move proved to be not a gamble but a milestone for the company, giving it the capacity to produce 100,000 barrels of beer a year. The site had its own railway sidings and was also close to the Trent & Mersey Canal: both train and canal gave the new company the opportunity to expand sales beyond the Midlands. In common with the brewers in central Burton, the railways proved a major boon for Marston's. In 1839 the Birmingham-Derby Junction Railway, later the Midland Railway, reached Burton, but the company that was most beneficial to Marston's was the North Staffordshire Railway – known as 'the Knotty' from the three-loop knot that is the symbol of Staffordshire – which linked Burton with Derby and, crucially, opened a halt at Horninglow. In 1878 the Great Northern built another link from Burton to Derby. With three train companies to choose from, Marston's could compete for the best rates of freight and was able to extend beer sales to London and the Home Counties.

Alfred Barnard, with his great eye for detail, had given a full description of the brewery when he visited during the ownership of Mann, Crossman & Paulin. Once again, the head brewer – in this case, Mr G.F. Cookson – was pressed into acting as the guide for Barnard and his team. 'The brewhouse, which contains four lofty storeys, is built with red brick and cement,' Barnard recorded, 'and each floor is reached by a spacious staircase, divided off by brick walls from the main building.' After visiting the malt store and grist cases, Barnard went down a floor and:

…we entered the mash room… measuring 50sqft, and of great height. Here we were shown two mash tuns, each with a cover constructed of pitch pine, and both commanded by a Steel's mashing machine. They are thirty-quarter tuns, and each is fitted with the usual sparger and draining plates. Crossing the mashing-room, we entered the copper stage, the floor of which is laid with iron plates. It is open to the roof, in which are placed ventilators to carry off the steam, and also contains louvred shutters for the same purpose.

Barnard next inspected the hop store, recording it was 'a noble chamber, which measures 100ft in length, and will contains upwards of 1,000 pockets [sacks]'. En route to the fermenting area, Barnard noted that:

…it is a speciality of this brewery that the celebrated Burton water, required for mashing, is always pumped direct from the wells into the heating vessels, and does not run from any reservoir. The two open coolers, to which the wort is pumped, are placed on the floor below; one of them a few feet above the other, and the lowest in direct communication with the refrigerators, to see which we followed our guide down stairs and into the fermenting department… This fermenting room, which measures 66ft by 40ft, contains twenty fermenting squares, the largest of which holds seventy barrels. Over the wide avenue between the vessels, and fixed on iron arches, is the copper main for conveying the wort from the refrigerators to the squares, so arranged, that it can be taken to pieces to be cleaned after each running-in. Underneath this floor is the union room, to which we next bent our steps. We thought the upper floor a large place, but this magnificent room somewhat astonished us. It is twice as large as the upper one, being the full width of the building, and extending underneath the whole floor of the hop-store. At one end there is a row of five cleansing squares, each holding 120 barrels, containing both attemperators and parachutes [parachutes are cones placed in the fermentation squares to collect yeast]. In front of them, and covering the whole floor, are numerous union casks with attemperated yeast troughs over them, all ranged on either side of seven wide avenues... Besides this union room, there are [an]other two, in another building in the yard, which we afterwards visited, containing together 96 union casks, all erected on iron frames, and containing attemperators.

The unions remain the central feature of Marston's production today. The use of trains has long gone and it's fascinating to read Barnard's description of the service designed for the brewery. Marston's in the twentieth century was still restless for further expansion. In 1901 it bought Beard, Hill & Co. of Lichfield Street, Burton – a brewery that dated from 1740 – followed by H.E. Ealand of Southwell in Nottinghamshire. In 1904 it added Wright's Crown Brewery of Market Drayton in Shropshire. But it was 1905 that saw the merger that is the most significant one of the period, for it formed Marston, Thompson & Evershed, the name by which the company was known for most of the twentieth century. Sydney Evershed was born in Surrey in 1825 and trained at Standsfield's Brewery in London before moving to Burton in 1854 where he bought the rundown Angel Inn. He restored the inn's fortunes and he also brewed on the site. He became a common brewer and by 1868 he owned two maltings as well as the flourishing brewery at Bank Square. He had much in common with the bigger brewers in the town. He played a leading role in the community and he was elected mayor in 1880 (following Worthington in the role) before becoming the Liberal MP for the Burton/Uttoxeter division between 1886 and 1900. When he died in 1903 he left the business, which included sixty-eight pubs, to his sons Percy and Sydney Herbert. The Bank Square site was cramped, with no room to expand, so the brothers decided to sell the business to Marston & Thompson for £260,000. Sydney Herbert Evershed was appointed a director of the new company and he became a national figure, excelling at cricket – he captained Derbyshire – and was an England Rugby international. At the annual shareholders' meeting in 1906, another director, Francis Thompson, said with the hyperbole typical of the time, that the merger had 'joined three of the oldest firms in the town, had lengthened their name, and like the great premier firm [Bass, Ratcliff and Gretton] in the town, I hope that some day we will do as well as that great triumvirate has done for many years past, and that our trademark might be held in the same great esteem all over the world.'

But unlike Bass, Marston's didn't build a world-wide reputation as it was not a great exporter of beer, preferring to build a solid domestic trade. Thompson's had brewed an India Pale Ale but that may have been solely for the English market. The brand seems to have disappeared following the amalgamation with Marston's: the records on beers brewed at the turn of the twentieth century are vague. It may at first seem remarkable that while all around the likes of Allsopp, Bass, Salt and Worthington had created large overseas sales for their pale ales, while Marston's was content to stay at home. But by the time the three breweries had created their new company in 1905, the great days of exported IPA were over. One beer that was recorded as a new brand in 1906 was Owd Rodger, which clearly identified Marston's Burton roots, for while it has been marketed variously as 'strong ale' or 'barley wine' it is, in effect, a fine example of a traditional Burton Ale. It's still brewed today, with a strength of 7.6 per cent, and is made with pale and crystal malts, glucose and caramel for colour, and hopped with Fuggles and Goldings. Nobody knows who 'Owd' [old] Rodger was. He's shown on bottle labels as a bucolic character with a hat, long clay pipe, cravat and glass of ale and he was not, as some believe, a brewery worker. It was rare at that time to give beers such a distinctive brand name: most draught beers were known simply by their cask marks, and Marston's pale ales were branded P, PX, PXX and PXXX. Many years later, P would blossom into one of the country's best-known beers. The quality of the company's beers received national recognition in 1912 and 1913, when it won gold cups for its bottled ales in the Brewers' Exhibition.

In common with all the Burton breweries, Marston's endured a torrid time in the First War One, with restrictions on beer strength, shortage of raw materials and reduced pub opening hours. Prime Minister David Lloyd George had predicted a fall in the beer trade of 35 per cent as a result of his restrictions but in fact trade fell even further than that figure. Marston's Derby Road maltings were requisitioned by the Ministry of Munitions and several brewery horses were commandeered for the war effort. Thirty-seven of Marston's employees were killed in action. The company was nevertheless quick to recover and was soon back on the takeover trail, buying Holmes of Wellington and Zachary Smith in Shardlow. The most significant acquisition came in 1923 when Marston's bought the Winchester Brewery in Hampshire. The brewery closed the following year but the site was kept as a warehouse and distribution centre. The 200 former Winchester pubs took Marston's beers, providing the company with an important stronghold in southern England that gave its beers a wide reputation usually reserved for the bigger Burton brewers.

Along with the rest of the industry, Marston's suffered from falling beer sales throughout the 1930s, a time of persistent high unemployment and economic gloom. While the Second World War, as we have seen, presented fewer problems

Marston's Pale Ale, for the second year in succession, was awarded the gold cup and the silver medal at the brewers' exhibition held in London in October 1913, for the best bottled beer in the show.

for brewers than the First World War, Marston's faced an ever-increasing rise in excise duty and a shortage of raw materials. When the war ended, the brewery withdrew some of its stronger beers as it felt it could not maintain their quality and distinctive character as a result of continuing shortages of malt and hops.

But as rationing ended and malt and hops became readily available once more, Marston's returned to full production and the directors took the decision to turn a pale ale simply known as P into Pedigree in 1954. Managing director Sydney Evershed said the beer was renamed 'because it is descended from a long line of famous brews and is really a thoroughbred'. Over the ensuing years, Pedigree has been marketed as bitter, but it's a true Burton pale ale, with a strength of 4.5 per cent and brewed in the true nineteenth century fashion with pale malt and glucose sugar, no coloured malts, and hopped with Fuggles and Goldings.

An equally fateful decision was taken in 1957 when Marston's allowed Whitbread to take a 10 per cent stake in the company. This was the start of Whitbread's 'umbrella scheme', whereby the big London brewer became a shareholder in a number of smaller regional producers to protect them against takeovers from unwelcome predators. In reality, Whitbread itself became a predator, a shark in the shallows, swallowing any smaller fish it could find. Most of the twenty-two breweries in which Whitbread took a stake in the 1960s were eventually taken over and closed. Whitbread turned itself into a national brewing and pub-owning colossus, able to compete on equal terms with the likes of the emerging Bass Charrington group. Marston's was one of the few 'umbrella' companies to survive Whitbread's cold embrace.

As a sign of the changing times, Marston's produced a range of keg beers, including Albion Mild, Albion Bitter and John Marston Premium Bitter, and introduced its own lager, called Pilsner Lager Bier. For drinkers concerned about their waistlines, it added Low Cal, a light ale with low carbohydrate content; it has remained a successful brand to this day, first renamed Low C and now labelled Resolution, but other keg beers eventually disappeared as demand for the style waned. In 1988 Pilsner Lager was discontinued as a result of a deal with Whitbread in which Marston's stocked Heineken and Stella Artois in its pubs while the national group took Pedigree as a premium cask ale in its large estate. The arrangement helped turn Pedigree into a national brand but it proved a double-edged sword: many Whitbread publicans had no experience of serving cask beer, certainly not one like Pedigree that requires time in the cellar to finish a secondary fermentation and 'drop bright'. Marston's later admitted that Pedigree's reputation suffered for a while as cloudy pints were dished up in Whitbread outlets.

The year 1984 was one of celebration for Marston's as it marked 100 years of brewing. A special bottled India Pale Ale was issued, while 170 pubs were added to the tied estate as a result of the takeover and closure of Border Breweries in

Wrexham: relations with CAMRA soured as the campaign condemned the snuffing out of a Welsh brewery, though most of its beers were keg. Marston's response was to point to its commitment to cask beer at a time when the Big Six national groups were reducing consumer choice by concentrating all their efforts on lager and turning their collective back on traditional ale. The point was underscored in the 1990s when a third union room of casks was installed at Burton at a cost of £1 million to keep pace with the ever-rising demand for Pedigree. But it seemed the Burton company, regardless of its commitment to cask beer, was in jeopardy in February 1999, when it was taken over by the major regional brewing group Wolverhampton & Dudley, or Wolves, as the group was known for short. The company was the result of a merger in 1890 of three Black Country breweries, with Julia Hanson's Dudley brewery added in 1943. The Dudley plant closed in 1991, with all production centralised at Banks's brewery in Wolverhampton. While Wolverhampton and Burton are geographically close, the beer traditions are sharply different: Burton's reputation is based on pale ale while the Black Country has long been the home of dark mild, a sweeter beer that pleased the palates of industrial workers in the region. Banks's best-selling beer, even in the twenty-first century, is mild and there were fears at the time of the takeover that Wolves lacked the sensitivity to appreciate the crucial importance of pale ale brewing to Burton. The 'worst case scenario' painted by critics of the merger was that Marston's would close, with production switched to Wolverhampton and the Burton unions becoming as redundant as those at Bass.

The fears were not justified. The name of the merged company was changed to Marston's and while the head office is now in Wolverhampton, brewing continues uninterrupted at Burton, with the unions given iconic status. As a result of the takeover, the Burton board became redundant. The chairman, Michael Hurdle, retired, ending his family's long association with the company. The impetus for the merger was the changing nature of the beer market. Large regional brewers – Wolves, Greene King, Fuller's and Charles Wells – were well aware they could not compete with the globally-owned national brewers who concentrated most of their resources on lager and new 'smooth flow' keg ales. With real ale enjoying a revival and CAMRA's membership and beer festivals booming, the regionals were determined to carve out an entirely different route to market as brewers of top-quality, premium cask beers. But the strategy required considerable investment, with brewing concentrated in key areas. While Greene King and Fuller's took over smaller breweries and closed them, and Charles Wells merged with Young's in London, Marston's followed a different strategy. Brakspear and Wychwood in Oxfordshire, Jennings in Cumbria and Ringwood in Hampshire were bought by Marston's but the breweries remain open and continue to supply their local areas. Marston's won considerable praise for its major investment in Jenning's when the brewery suffered severe damage during the Cumbrian floods in 2009, forcing it to close for three months. Most pundits expected Jenning's to shut permanently but Marston's immediately announced it would repair the site at a cost of several million pounds.

In the twenty-first century, Marston's at last added a Burton IPA to its regular portfolio. Old Empire, available in cask and bottle, is 5.7 per cent and is brewed with Optic pale malt, Fuggles and Goldings hops, with American Cascade as a late hop for a delicious citrus note. In 2009, Marston's widened the scope of Pedigree and other cask beers by developing a new yeast system known as Fast Cask. Instead of adding liquid yeast to casks for secondary fermentation, yeast is turned by a natural – though confidential system – into yeast 'beads'. While a natural secondary fermentation still takes place, the beads drop almost immediately to the foot of the cask. If a cask is disturbed and the yeast shaken up, the beer will drop bright straight away instead of waiting several hours to clear using a conventional method. Fast Cask has allowed real ale to be made available to sports grounds, trains, ships and clubs that would not normally consider taking live beer. Traditional cask beer with liquid yeast is still available to mainstream pubs.

Today Marston's is a large national group with 2,200 pubs and 3,000 free trade accounts. At Burton, head brewer Emma Gilleland – a brewster – produces some 250,000 barrels a year. As we shall see in the next chapter, small craft breweries are blossoming in Burton, but Marston's is the last brewery in the town with its roots in the nineteenth century, proudly using the union system that transformed pale-ale brewing in Victorian England.

Chapter Nine

BURTON REBORN

Brewing has returned to Burton in a small but encouraging fashion. The first new brewery in the town, Burton Bridge, was founded in 1982 at a historic junction: the foot of the seventeenth-century bridge across the Trent and opposite the site of Benjamin Printon's brewery, the first commercial beer maker in the town. John Thompson, Boddingtons, Salt and John Nunneley all once brewed within 150 yards of the Burton Bridge Inn.

The inn was first called the Fox & Goose and it was bought by Bass in the nineteenth century from the Marquis of Anglesey. It closed in 1982. Geoff Mumford drove across the bridge one day, saw the 'for sale' sign outside the pub and thought, as there was plenty of space at the back, it would make the ideal shop window for a small craft brewery.

Geoff and Bruce Wilkinson both worked for Allied Breweries as senior managers at Ind Coope in Burton and Romford. Geoff was an engineering manager and Bruce a technical manager. 'We were heads of departments,' Geoff says, 'and in the 1980s we could see the writing on the wall. Allied had closed Ansells in Birmingham and Romford was treated like the Siberia of brewing. We knew it would shut so we decided to jump ship.'

They thought it would be feasible to make a living by brewing on a small scale with the pub attached: 'It wouldn't have worked without the pub,' they say. On the advice of their accountants, they formed a partnership rather than a limited company. The business remains a partnership today but 'we've stopped calling ourselves partners in case we get funny looks': they're both married with families.

They chose Burton because of its central position in England, a handy base for getting malt and hops, and the home of specialist manufacturers of brewing equipment: the major firm of Briggs, which builds breweries as far away as Australia, has its factory in the town. The partners' first beer was Bridge Bitter. Unlike the cheap materials used at Ind Coope, Bruce and Geoff bought the finest Maris Otter malting barley along with Challenger and Target hops and they used Styrian Goldings from Slovenia to 'dry hop' the beer in cask for additional aroma and flavour.

The early years of the partnership proved to be punishing hard work. Bruce and Geoff would start work at 7 a.m., brew beer, go out and deliver it, then return at around 5 p.m. to take over running the pub from a daytime manager. They regularly worked a seven-day week. Today they employ a staff of eleven, though they still take a hand at delivering beer within a 35-miles radius of Burton, which takes in Birmingham, Leicester, Nottingham and Stoke-on-Trent. Specialist wholesalers distribute the beers further afield. Their extensive beer range includes Sovereign Gold, XL Bitter, Burton Porter, Stairway to Heaven, Top Dog Stout, Festival Ale and Thomas Sykes. There are also monthly seasonal beers. The Burton Bridge interpretation of IPA is a bottled beer called Empire Pale Ale that was first brewed in 1996 and just one year later won the *Guardian* newspaper's award for Best Bottle-Conditioned Beer. The following year it was runner-up in a joint Guardian/CAMRA competition. Empire Pale Ale is a faithful recreation of a Victorian IPA, using just pale malt and invert sugar, with Challenger and Styrian Goldings. The beer is matured in cask for six months to replicate the long sea voyage to India in the nineteenth century. It's then dry hopped with Styrians and primed with additional brewing sugar to encourage a second fermentation in bottle. The beer (7.5 per cent) has a pronounced orange fruit note from the hops and yeast culture, the fruitiness balanced by biscuity malt and a deep tangy, spicy hop resins, ending with a long finish packed with juicy malt, tart fruit and bitter hop notes. The striking label shows an officer of the Raj and a cricketer quaffing tankards of ale.

Burton Bridge has won many other awards in competitions staged by both CAMRA and the Society of Independent Brewers (SIBA). While its beers are sold widely throughout the country, the partners have remained true to their Burton roots by building an estate of five pubs in the town: Bridge Inn, Devonshire Arms, Great Northern, Plough and Prince Alfred. When Bruce and Geoff started their pub-and-brewery business, they brewed 800 barrels a year. Today the figure is 3,000 barrels and the brewery behind the pub is now a large enterprise. They could easily expand production due to the demand for their beers but the burden of excise duty stops them. In 2002, the government brought in Progressive Beer Duty, a scheme designed to help smaller brewers pay less duty. It has been of enormous benefit to the craft brewing sector, but the scheme has a ceiling of 60,000 hectolitres a year and includes a 'taper': the closer a brewery gets to the ceiling, the more duty it pays, so there's an incentive to stay well below the cut-off point.

The former Salt's water tower, now home of Tower Brewery.

So Bruce and Geoff are content to stay small, happy in the knowledge that, following the carnage of the last half of the twentieth century, they have helped restore Burton's brewing heritage.

It's impossible to move in Burton without coming across the brewing history of the town. John Mills at Tower Brewery is surrounded – steeped is a better word – by history as he's based in the former water tower of Thomas Salt's malting. The building is in the Walsitch area of Burton. Walsitch is a name from the Anglo-Saxon period and means a stream that acted as a boundary. John Mills worked as a brewer at Burton Bridge for ten years before he decided to branch out on his own. He opened his brewery in 2001 and as a result of his painstaking work was given an award by the Civic Society for the restoration of a Historic Industrial Building. The top floor of the building, reached by narrow spiral stairs and walk-ways, is heavily beamed and contains the original water tanks used by Salt's, which had three maltings in the town. As the windows in the top floor were broken, John's conversion of the building began with the daunting task of shovelling some four tons of pigeon droppings into sacks and dropping them down to the ground floor. He then had to encourage the large number of birds to leave the building, which is now pigeon-free as a result of replacing the windows. The depth of the droppings was measured by the fact that some of the beams were hidden from view. Now they can be inspected and there are two fascinating inscriptions: 'T.S. [Thomas Salt] 1875' and 'Alf Tyler – maltster 1957'.

The ground floor is occupied by modern brewing vessels – mash tuns and coppers – with fermenters in a back room. Some of the vessels are second-hand, others were built by a local engineering firm. John brews some 12,000 barrels a year, which makes him a sizeable small craft producer. His main beers all make a deep bow in the direction of Burton's history: Salt's Burton Ale, Gone for a Burton, Tower Bitter, Malty Towers and Imperial IPA. He has built his business by brewing for other companies and pubs. He produces Sheriff's Tipple for Castle Rock Brewery in Nottingham, six beers for Hoskins Brother in Leicester (Hobs Best Mild, Brigadier Bitter, Hob Bitter, Tom Kelly's Stout, White Dolphin and EXS) and for the Steamin' Billy Brewing Co. in Oadby, Leicestershire, Last Bark, Scrum Down, Rat Tosser, Bitter and Skydiver. John also produces house beers for several pubs and has twenty outlets for his own beers. In May 2011, John opened a small reception centre called the Sample Room at the brewery where visitors can enjoy a glass or two of his beers and study the fascinating memorabilia of Burton and its brewing on the walls and shelves.

Black Hole is another brewery enveloped by history. It's based in the former Ind Coope Bottling Hall and the scale of the Ind Coope business can be measured by the fact that a dozen or more small businesses now occupy the site on what is today called the Imex Business Park. Black Hole has been running since 2007 and, according to Martin Hodson, who brews with Jack Morgan, the name was chosen because 'there's an infinite number of beer names you can choose around the black hole theme'. The brewery slogan is 'Beers that are out this world', and the theme is underscored by such brand names as Cosmic, Red Dwarf, Supernova, No Escape and Milky Way, as well as the more down-to-earth Bitter. The brewing plant is second hand and can produce ten barrels at a time. Martin and Jack brew three times a week and plan to install additional fermenting vessels to keep pace with demand. They supply around 300 outlets, including the Wetherspoons group as well as pubs run by Titanic Brewery in Stoke-on-Trent, while wholesalers distribute the beers further afield.

Burton Old Cottage Brewery was first based in the former Heritage Brewery, originally owned by Everards (when the Leicester company had a second brewery in Burton) and built in the middle of the nineteenth century. When the Heritage site was sold, Old Cottage moved to a new industrial estate, the Eccleshall Business Park on Hawkins Lane. Old Cottage takes its name from the Old Cottage Tavern in Byrkley Street, behind Burton Town Hall, which had a tiny brewery for a short time. When brewing stopped, the name was adopted by four partners – John Saville, Mick Machin, his brother Dave, and Paul Wakelin – when they launched their enterprise in 2006.

The brewing operation is part-time. John Saville worked in computing and retired in 2006 but his wife encouraged him to join the other three partners in running Old Cottage. The Machin brothers work for Molson Coors and help out at Old Cottage on their days off. They produce 200 barrels of beer a year, most of which is sold through the Old Cottage Tavern. Twenty more pubs are supplied and the partners have invested in additional brewing equipment as demand increases.

'We struggle to make sufficient beer for the Old Cottage,' John Saville said, 'and we need to employ a salesman to develop beer sales further afield.' The beers include Oak Ale, Cottage IPA, Stout, Halcyon Daze, Cloughy's Clout, Chestnut Beer and Redwood, while the partners plan to add a barley wine. Tours of the brewery can be arranged, with the beers sampled in an attractive upstairs lounge that has a bar, comfortable seating and old brewery memorabilia.

An illustrious name has been restored to the town with the opening of William Worthington's Brewery as part of the National Brewery Centre in the Molson Coors complex. Visitors to the centre can watch beer being brewed on the 22.5-barrel plant run by Steve Wellington and Jo White. Steve has been brewing for various parts of the Bass and now Molson Coors empires since the 1960s and for several years ran the White Shield Brewery that produced Worthington's White Shield and special brews such as P2 Stout and Bass No 1. The success of White Shield in recent years led to the beer being moved into the main Molson Coors brewery. Steve and Jo lobbied hard for the brewing giant to install new equipment within the re-opened visitor centre as a tourist attraction. Following protracted negotiations, Molson Coors agreed to invest £1 million in the new brewery, which opened in December 2010, with five times the capacity of the old White Shield plant.

Steve Wellington knew he wanted to brew when, as a boy, he smelt the delightful piny and spicy aroma of Northdown hops in Cobbs Brewery in Margate, Kent, long ago closed by Whitbread. The White Shield plant in Burton was originally designed as a pilot brewery to try out new recipes at the Mitchells & Butlers brewery in Birmingham. In December 2010, Steve and Jo moved across the cobbled yard to the new plant, built by a local firm, Grange Engineering. Steve would have preferred to brew in wood but costs dictated that the new equipment should be made from metal. Remarkably, it's an ale-only brewery in a vast complex where Molson Coors concentrates on producing large volumes of Carling and Grolsch lagers. The reason the global brewer agreed to invest in the new plant was that it was aware that cask ale is the only sector of the brewing industry showing a small sign of growth. To date, Steve and Jo have produced a cask-conditioned version of Worthington E, once one of the infamous keg beers of the 1970s, a draught version of White Shield and a new cask beer, Red Shield, designed for national distribution. There are also regular seasonal beers such as spring, autumn and winter beers called Shield.

Older Bass beers have not been neglected, and P2 Stout and Bass No. 1 are also produced in small batches from time to time, helping to maintain a link with Burton's past. In May 2011, Molson Coors reported that the Worthington brewery had produced more beer in the first quarter of the year than in the whole of 2010. It's on course to make 3,000 barrels a year and the giant national pub company Mitchells & Butlers has taken several of its beers. Steve Wellington was due to retire in 2011 and he will leave a proud record of his dedication to brewing.

Useful Contacts

Black Hole Brewery Ltd, Unit 63, Imex Business Park, Shobnall Road, DE14 2AU; 01283 534060; blackholebrewery.co.uk

Burton Bridge Brewery, 24 Bridge Street, DE14 1SY. 01283 510573; burtonbridgebrewery.co.uk.

Burton Old Cottage Beer Co. Ltd, Unit 10, Eccleshall Business Park, Hawkins Lane, DE14 1PT. 07909 931250; oldcottagebeer.co.uk

Tower Brewery, Old Water Tower, Walsitch Maltings, Glensyl Way, DE14 1LX. 01283 530695.

William Worthington's Brewery, National Brewery Centre, Horninglow Street, DE14 1NG. 01283 532 880; nationalbrewerycentre.co.uk.

Chapter Ten

THE FIGHT FOR
THE MUSEUM

The fascinating history of brewing in Burton is told in a museum based in the former Bass buildings on Horninglow Street. Museum is a word that conjures up images of dust, cobwebs and static displays under glass – an image the owners are anxious to dispel. What was the Bass Museum is now the National Brewery Centre and it contains working models, interactive displays, live actors, dray horses and, as described in the previous chapter, the William Worthington Brewery.

It seemed in 2008 that this treasure trove of Burton's brewing heritage would be lost. The Bass Museum opened in 1977 in the three-storey, Grade II-listed former joiners' shop. At its peak, the museum attracted 120,000 visitors a year who could follow the history of brewing in the town from the days of the abbey to the twentieth century, with particular emphasis on the expansion of the nineteenth century as a result of the demand for India Pale Ale.

When Bass left brewing and the entire brewing complex passed to the American brewer Coors, the museum was under-promoted and visitor numbers fell. In 2008, Coors announced the museum was losing £1 million a year and the company had decided to close it. There was outrage not only in Burton at the decision but also throughout the brewing industry and among historians and lovers of beer. Within days, the Member of Parliament for Burton, Janet Dean, convened a meeting in the town to discuss the possibility of saving the museum. The meeting was attended by representatives of the local Civic Society and Chamber of Commerce, the borough and county councils, Staffordshire Arts and Museums, the editor of

Worthington truck on view at National Brewery Centre.

the *Burton Mail*, the Campaign for Real Ale and the British Guild of Beer Writers. There was a unanimous determination to save the museum and maintain it as a focal point in the town and the region. A task group was set up to look into several options for the centre, including turning it into a trust that could seek National Heritage Lottery Funding.

Feelings were running high in Burton and Derby. The *Burton Mail*, a daily paper, highlighted the campaign to save the centre and there was considerable media coverage when CAMRA organised a 400-strong demonstration through the town and past the museum. Against the wishes of their employer, Coors workers lined the pavement to watch the march go past and brought out the famous Bass dray horses to stand alongside them. In far away Boulder, Colorado, Coors was horrified by the bad publicity. Senior executives flew to Britain and told the local management – in no uncertain terms – to sort out the problem.

Meanwhile, the task group set up by Janet Dean met on a regular basis to discuss tactics. Experts told the group that heritage lottery funding could take several years to obtain and the chances of getting funding for the museum were slim, as a large donation had just been given to restore the Wedgwood Pottery Museum in nearby Stoke-on-Trent. Janet Dean used her parliamentary credentials to arrange a meeting for the task group with Margaret Hodge MP, Minister of State for Culture and Tourism in the Labour government. Mrs Hodge agreed to write to every brewery in Britain, asking them if they would be prepared to give financial

The Burton Cooper, a bronze statue in Cooper Square, erected in 1977 and designed by James Butler RA. It was commissioned by Burton Civic Society.

backing to a fund to enable the museum to be saved and re-opened. But unknown to Janet Dean and the task group, events were moving fast back in Burton. They were asked to attend a meeting at Molson Coors – as the group had become – in November 2009 where they were told the brewer had reached an agreement with the leisure company Planning Solutions to take over the site. Planning Solutions, founded by Mike Stickland who had previously worked for the Rank Organisation, had the right credentials for the job. It runs the highly successful Conkers family venue in the National Forest, had previously been involved in the Robin Hood visitor attraction in Nottingham and had a role in Vinopolis, the London wine centre.

Molson Coors made an initial donation of £200,000 to the new centre and will make an annual contribution of £100,000. Mike Stickland believes that as more people are taking holidays in Britain rather than abroad, visitor attractions can draw greater numbers. As well as the visitor centre, the complex includes a bar with an attractive garden, a large restaurant, and rooms for hire that are suitable for meetings, conferences and wedding receptions. While he hopes the museum will make a small profit, he expects the other areas to generate most income.

There was a flurry of activity between November 2009 and April 2010 when the centre reopened. Many of the old displays remained, including the story of IPA and a recreation of the Bass laboratory in the nineteenth century, where brewing scientists such as Cornelius O'Sullivan improved the quality of beer. Additions include interactive presentations and actors representing all levels of the industry in Victorian times, from great entrepreneurs to maltsters and coopers.

There was a formal opening of the centre in September, conducted by Princess Anne, who had officiated at the launch of the original Bass Museum in 1977.

Finally, as seen in the previous chapter, Molson Coors added the William Worthington Brewery to the complex at the end of the year. The beers from the brewery are on tap in the centre's bar and can also be enjoyed with meals in the restaurant.

Thanks to the vigorous campaign spearheaded by Janet Dean, who retired at the 2010 general election, Burton has restored a museum that presents a dynamic image of a historic brewing town now reshaping itself for the future.

Recreation of the Bass laboratory in the nineteenth century.

Chapter Eleven

THE BEER THAT CAME
IN FROM THE COLD

In the autumn of 2010, a remarkable find was made in the cellars of the former
Allsopps brewery across the road from Burton railway station. The building had
been used for the best part of ten years by the pub groups Punch Taverns and Spirit,
but it was being renovated in preparation for being turned into apartments with
a leisure centre in the cellars. The new owner of the site, Kamran Khazai, found
a collection of old bottles of beer stored in crates in the cellar, covered in dust
and cobwebs. He contacted local people with an interest in beer, including May
Arthur of the local branch of the Campaign for Real Ale, and research identified
the beer as samples of Allsopps Arctic Ale.

   The discovery created enormous interest among beer connoisseurs, not least an
American called Chris Bowen, who happened to be visiting Burton at the time
and was allowed to take a few bottles back to the United States. He planned to
have the beer and yeast scientifically analysed in order to brew a batch of his own
Arctic Ale.

   Allsopps Arctic Ale was brewed in 1875 and it's a beer interwoven with both
history and tragedy. In 1845 Rear-Admiral Sir John Franklin led an expedition to
the Canadian Arctic in an attempt to chart and navigate the North West Passage
from the Atlantic to the Pacific. Such a passage had for centuries been considered of
enormous potential benefit to the world's trading nations, as it would substantially
reduce sailing times. Franklin's mission failed. The ships foundered and were lost,
and the crew perished. There were rumours spread by Inuits in the Arctic of

Bottles of Arctic Ale, briefly recreated in the twentieth century.

cannibalism among the crew, but this was hushed up in Victorian Britain. On the contrary, Franklin became a national hero and Queen Victoria demanded that efforts be made to find any remains of his ships and crew. Along with the Admiralty, the queen asked brewers in Burton, with their experience of making strong beer for export, to create 'life sustaining ale' to supply five ships commanded by Sir Edward Belcher: beers such as Burton Ale contain high levels of vitamin B that can help prevent scurvy.

Belcher led an expedition in 1851 but failed to find any trace of Franklin's ships or crew. Bass, Salt, Truman and Worthington had all competed to produce a beer for Belcher but the contract was awarded to Allsopps. Two bottles of Arctic Ale from 1851 exist but they are in the United States. In 1857, Allsopps again brewed the beer for a second search for the Franklin expedition, led by Sir Leopold McClintock. He was also unsuccessful and, as far as anyone knows, no bottles from that batch exist. But Arctic Ale was brewed yet again in 1875 for Sir George Nares's expedition to locate the North Pole and it was beers from the batch that were found in the Allsopp's cellars in 2010.

In February 2011, a small group of nervous and excited beer lovers met in the bar of the National Brewery Centre in Burton. They included May Arthur, Jason Potts (who had liaised closely with Chris Bowen in the U.S.), Steve Wellington from the William Worthington Brewery and the author. Jason arrived clutching a bottle of Arctic Ale as though his life depended on it, while Steve held two bottles of beer and a special corkscrew designed to remove old and damaged corks. Steve's presence was vital, as he was in possession of many old bottles of Bass ales dating from the nineteenth and early twentieth centuries and he was adept in storing, opening and decanting them. The two beers he brought to the tasting for comparison were Arctic Global Warmer, a 15 per cent modern recreation of the style brewed by Jon Pilling at the North Cotswold Brewery in Warwickshire, and a

Bass King's Ale dating from the coronation of Edward VII in 1902. The King's Ale is based on Bass No. 1, a strong interpretation of Burton Ale.

Jon Pilling's Global Warmer is one of the strongest beers brewed in Britain and is made with pale, crystal and chocolate malts, roasted barley and wheat malt and hopped with Challenger, Fuggles and Goldings hops. It had a fresh tobacco aroma with a yeasty/Marmite note, with sweet malt in the mouth, hints of treacle, dark chocolate, vinous fruit and spicy hops. The finish was bittersweet with soft, rich malt, burnt fruit and hops. As he removed the cork from the bottle of King's Ale, Steve Wellington said it was 10.5 per cent alcohol and was an all-malt beer, with no added brewing sugar, plus six pounds of Fuggles and Goldings hops – that's an enormous level of hops. Only pale malt was used, and the deep amber/tawny colour was the result of a twelve-hour boil during which time some of the malt sugars turned to caramel. It was wonderfully drinkable, with a massive vinous fruit aroma similar to Madeira, followed by more rich fruit in the mouth with a hint of peppery hops, and a dry finish with molasses, caramel, toffee, burnt fruit and light hops.

Then came the moment of truth. With enormous care and skill, Steve delicately turned the screw into the cork of Allsopp's Arctic Ale. As he started to draw the cork, there was a sharp intake of breath from all involved as the cork began to disintegrate and Steve warned us that there was a possibility the beer might have suffered from oxidation. The remains of the cork were finally removed and Steve poured small samples into glasses. The beer was dark amber in colour and had an astonishingly complex aroma of dry chocolate, cocoa powder, molasses and vinous fruit. The palate offered creamy malt, sweet fruit and further hints of chocolate and cocoa, followed by a bittersweet finish with dark fruit, rich and slightly roasted grain and further chocolate and cocoa hints, with only the faintest hint of hops. Frustratingly, no information about the recipe has survived, but it's likely only pale malt was used along with Fuggles and Goldings, the dominant hop varieties of the time. Astonishingly, the beer had survived in fine drinkable condition and had not suffered from oxidation. The tasters were unanimous that, 136 years old, it was the best beer of the three. Another piece of the Burton jigsaw had clicked into place.

In the U.S., Chris Bowen's work on Arctic Ale created considerable interest, including a report in the *New York Times*. Chris has brewed five batches of the beer, including one on the shore of Hudson Bay in Canada. He used malt from Thomas Fawcett in Yorkshire, hops and yeast from the Yakima Valley in Washington State – Goldings and Wyeast, a culture ideal for making English barley wine – and Canadian water from the Ruppert River.

GOING FOR A BURTON

The Otley Brewery in Pontypridd, south Wales, may seem an odd location to brew a special Burton Ale but, as this book has shown, 'brewing a Burton' was almost a national obsession when the style was in its prime in the nineteenth century. The brewery, owned by three brothers, Nick, Charlie and Matthew Otley, opened in 2005, has doubled in size, and has been such a success that new and bigger premises are being sought. They produce 3,200 barrels a year, plan to increase that figure to 4,000 and will install new conditioning tanks. As well as such regular beers as O1, Dark O, O2, O-Garden, OG and O8, the brothers are keen to recreate old beer styles and were happy to accept the challenge to brew a Burton for this book. Time restraints meant the beer had to be a 'New Burton' of medium strength as an 'Old Burton' would have needed several months' maturation. The beer, called O-Roger, was based on Ind Coope Draught Burton Ale, which in turn was a cask-conditioned version of bottled Double Diamond.

On 31 March 2011, Matt Otley started preparations for the brew at 9 a.m. He was joined by Arielle Rovati – known as Harry – an Italian beer lover who had come to Britain to learn the skills of brewing. The recipe was based on pale malt, English Fuggles and Goldings hops, with the American hop Columbus as a late addition to the hop boil. As the beer could have only a relatively short time to mature, it was decided to add a small amount of amber malt to the pale for both colour and 'mouthfeel', to give the finished the beer the roundness and rich malt character of Burton Ale.

The beer had a starting or original gravity of 1,054 degrees and the aim was for a finished strength of 5.2 per cent alcohol, with 50 units of bitterness. That's a high level of bitterness: 30 to 35 would be more typical of strong British ale. Otley brewed 820 litres or five barrels of beer and the ingredients were made up of 145 kilograms of pale malt, 8.5kg of amber, with 1,113 grams of Fuggles, 1,411 grams of Goldings and 2,525 grams of Columbus. The brewing liquor or water was 'Burtonised' with the addition of salts. The yeast culture used was called Nottingham: despite the name, it originates in Canada and is popular with small brewers with limited space as it creates less of a frothy head as the beer ferments.

While Harry filled the mash tun with boiling water, Matt poured sacks of malt into a hopper above the tun. The water was 80 degrees C and this would be brought down to a 'strike temperature' of 71.5 degrees – if the water was too hot it would kill the enzymes in the malt. By 9.40 a.m. the hopper was filled with the required amount of malt. Matt opened the base of the hopper and the grain poured down into the mash tun. Immediately, a rich and enticing aroma of freshly-baked biscuits and wholemeal bread filled the air. The mash would take one hour and fifteen minutes, and during that time the natural enzymes in the malt would convert starch to sugar. The grain lowered the temperature of the mash to 65 degrees, the level at which starch conversion can take place. Harry vigorously stirred the mash, which became thicker and took on the consistency and colour of porridge.

At 11.20 a.m. Harry and Matt started the 'run off' – the transfer of the liquid now known as wort from the mash tun to the copper. The wort flows from the tun into a receiving vessel and from there along a pipe into the copper. At the same time, the grain left in the tun is 'sparged': perforated arms in the roof of the vessel rotate and spray the grain with a shower of hot water to wash out any remaining malt sugars. Harry handed me a glass with a sample of the wort. It was cloudy and bronze coloured with a touch of red from the amber malt. It was warm and biscuity to the taste, like Weetabix with muscles.

Matt brought Fuggles and Goldings from the hop store into the brew house. He poured small amounts of both varieties into the copper before the boil starts as this allows for maximum extraction of the oils, resins and tannins from the plants. The Fuggles are pale yellow and green, with a spicy, tobacco-like aroma while the Goldings are greener with a gentle, fruity aroma. Two bucket-loads of the hops were poured into the copper and thoroughly mixed with the wort. The temperature in the copper was 70 degrees but this would be raised to 100 to 105 degrees as a good rolling boil took place. The boil would last for two hours and during that time the oils, resins and tannins would be extracted, adding delightful aromas and flavours of spice, pepper and citrus fruit to the wort. The extracts also act as a powerful protection against bacterial infection of the wort.

It was 1 p.m., a good time to repair to one of Otley's three pubs in Pontypridd, the Bunch of Grapes, for lunch. Harry and Matt were joined by Nick, who had been organising sales from his office above the brewery, and Charlie, who had been delivering beer to pubs. Food was accompanied by only a modicum of beer – in Charlie's case, just a soft drink – as clear heads were needed for the rest of the working day. Back at the brewery, the copper boil continued: it was at least half an hour longer than a normal boil, as the lengthy process would 'caramelise' some of the brewing sugar, helping to give the finished beer the correct Burton colour and character. By 3.15 p.m. it was time to start the run off. As the liquid, now called 'hopped wort', started to drain from the bottom of the copper, Matt added Columbus hops at the top; the American variety was a richer green than the English ones and had a delightful piny and pungent citrus aroma. By 3.50 p.m. the run off was complete. Matt opened the front of the copper to reveal a great bed of steaming spent hops still bursting with aroma. The used grain and hops are supplied to farmers as fertiliser and animal feed.

I was given a further taste of the emerging beer. The hopped wort had an orange/russet colour with, again, a rich biscuit aroma and flavour, but now with an intense bitterness that was almost quinine or iodine-like. Matt assured me some of this hop bitterness would soften during fermentation.

The hopped wort was cooled by passing through a paraflow, a sort of double radiator with cold water running alongside panels containing the hot liquid. The paraflow cools the liquid in preparation for fermentation. At 4 p.m. it was time for the hopped wort to meet its destiny. It was pumped into the fermenting vessel and Matt poured in liquid yeast from a bucket and then stirred it into the wort. There was no more that human activity could achieve. As Fritz Maytag, owner of the Anchor Brewery in San Francisco, aptly puts it: 'We assemble the raw ingredients the best we can then stand back and let nature do the rest.'

Fermentation would last for a week and the beer would then be stored in cask to mature.

A month later, a bottle containing a sample of the beer reached me. This, Nick Otley was keen to stress, was work in progress and the beer would continue to mature for several more weeks. Nevertheless, I poured the beer with a degree of reverence and excitement. It was unfiltered, with live yeast in the bottle. O-Roger had a hazy bronze colour and a massive aroma of fresh tobacco and a rich fruitiness reminiscent of peaches and strawberries, balanced by lightly toasted grain and spicy hops. Tart and bitter hops built in the mouth, balanced by rich malt and bittersweet fruit. The finish was amazingly complex, with bitter hop resins and lingering hints of tart fruit, tobacco and juicy malt. It was, in short, a wonderful beer. The next step was to allow the beer to continue to mature and then launch it in Burton-on-Trent. This happened on 12 July when Burton

Bridge Brewery generously allowed Nick Otley to serve O-Roger in two of their pubs, the Devonshire Arms and the Prince Alfred, the first opposite the Molson Coors complex, formerly Bass, the second across the road from where the Truman Brewery once stood.

The beer was now more than three months old. Served on draught, it had changed in depth and character considerably from the bottled sample. It had a bright amber colour and the aroma burst with tangy and spicy hop resins, juicy malt and rich fruit. The palate was a complex balance of spicy hops, biscuity malt and ripe fruit, with a long, full-bodied finish ending bittersweet from malt and hops. Amazingly, magically, all the way from South Wales we had the colour, aroma and palate of a true Burton.

Nick and Matthew Otley then pulled a rabbit from the hat: they produced a second version of O-Roger. This was a 'dry hopped' beer, which means that additional hops were added to the cask for aroma and palate. They had used two American hops, Aurora and Galena, and the 'nose' on the beer was quite astonishing: peppery, spicy, floral and a hint of fresh tobacco. This version had even more depth and customers in the pubs had the unusual pleasure of sampling two versions of the same beer and deciding which they preferred.

Sources and Further Reading

Anonymous, *A Glass of Pale Ale* (Wyman & Sons, 1880)

Barnard, A., *Noted Breweries of Great Britain and Ireland* (4 volumes) (Causton & Sons, 1889-91)

Bickerdyke, J., *The Curiosities of Ale and Beer* (Swann Sonnenschein, 1889)

Brown, P., *Hops and Glory* (Macmillan, 2009)

Cornell, M., *Beer: the Story of the Pint* (Headline, 2003)

Corran, H.S., *A History of Brewing* (David & Charles, 1975)

Fraser, A., *Mary Queen of Scots* (Weidenfeld & Nicolson, 1969)

Gourvish, T.R., and Wilson, R.G., *The British Brewing Industry, 1830-1980*, (Cambridge University Press, 1994)

Hawkins, K., *A History of Bass Charrington* (Oxford, 1978)

Hobsbawm, E., *Industry and Empire* (Penguin, 1968)

Mathias, P., *The Brewing Industry in England, 1700-1830* (Cambridge University Press, 1959)

Molyneux, William, *Burton-on-Trent: Its History, Its Waters, and Its Breweries* (Trübner & Co, 1869)

Owen, Colin C., *The Greatest Brewery in the World: a History of Bass, Ratcliff & Gretton* (Derbyshire Record Society, 1992)

La Pensée, C. and Protz, R., *Home Brew Classics: India Pale Ale* (CAMRA Books, 2001)

Protz, R., *The Great British Beer Book* (Impact Books, 1992)

Stone, R., *Burton upon Trent: a History* (Phillimore, 2004)

INDEX